R. T. Kendall is a brilliant theologian and man of the Spirit. With balanced and exegetical precision he has given us a complete and very readable guide to how the Holy Spirit works in our lives. Read a chapter every day and follow up with the included prayers and verses, and you will not only learn more about who the Holy Spirit is but also—more importantly—come to know Him in a whole new way. I believe that this book could greatly inspire your heart and change your life.

—MIKE BICKLE
INTERNATIONAL HOUSE OF PRAYER OF KANSAS CITY

Dr. Kendall writes as a theologian who knows the Holy Spirit, but who knows better than to try to tame Him. So you will find helpful things in this book that other works on the Holy Spirit ignore. He writes with the heart of a pastor. So he is not content to offer only a cogent explanation of what it means to blaspheme the Holy Spirit. He offers this consolation to those tormented by the thought that they have committed the unpardonable sin: "If you can say in your heart of hearts, 'Jesus is Lord,' it is because you have the Holy Spirit. You have not blasphemed Him."

—JACK DEERE

D0106608

40 Days
with the
HOLY SPIRIT

*A journey to experience His presence
in a fresh new way*

R.T. KENDALL

CHARISMA
HOUSE

Most CHARISMA HOUSE BOOK GROUP products are available at special quantity discounts for bulk purchase for sales promotions, premiums, fund-raising, and educational needs. For details, write Charisma House Book Group, 600 Rinehart Road, Lake Mary, Florida 32746, or telephone (407) 333-0600.

FORTY DAYS WITH THE HOLY SPIRIT by R. T. Kendall
Published by Charisma House
Charisma Media/Charisma House Book Group
600 Rinehart Road
Lake Mary, Florida 32746
www.charismahouse.com

This book or parts thereof may not be reproduced in any form, stored in a retrieval system, or transmitted in any form by any means—electronic, mechanical, photocopy, recording, or otherwise—without prior written permission of the publisher, except as provided by United States of America copyright law.

Unless otherwise noted, all Scripture quotations are from the Holy Bible, New International Version. Copyright © 1973, 1978, 1984, International Bible Society. Used by permission.

Scripture quotations marked ESV are from the Holy Bible, English Standard Version. Copyright © 2001 by Crossway Bibles, a division of Good News Publishers. Used by permission.

Scripture quotations marked KJV are from the King James Version of the Bible.

Scripture quotations marked NIRV are taken from the Holy Bible, New International Reader's Version. Copyright © 1996, 1998 Biblica. All rights reserved throughout the world. Used by permission of Biblica.

Scripture quotations marked NKJV are from the New King James Version of the Bible. Copyright © 1979, 1980, 1982 by Thomas Nelson, Inc., publishers. Used by permission.

Copyright © 2014 by R. T. Kendall
All rights reserved

Cover design by Bill Johnson

Visit the author's website at www.rtkendallministries.com.

Library of Congress Cataloging-in-Publication Data:
Kendall, R. T.
  Forty days with the Holy Spirit / R. T. Kendall. -- First edition.
       pages cm
  Includes bibliographical references.
  ISBN 978-1-62136-977-6 (trade paper) -- ISBN 978-1-62136-978-3 (ebook)
  1. Holy Spirit. I. Title.
  BT121.3.K453 2014
  231'.3--dc23
                                    2014002753

While the author has made every effort to provide accurate telephone numbers and Internet addresses at the time of publication, neither the publisher nor the author assumes any responsibility for errors or for changes that occur after publication.

Portions of this book were previously published in *Holy Fire* by R. T. Kendall, copyright © 2014, published by Charisma House, ISBN 978-1-62136-604-1.

20 21 22 23 24 — 13 12 11 10 9
Printed in the United States of America

To Toby and Timothy

Contents

PREFACE

I WAS SURPRISED BUT delighted that my publisher asked me to write this book—*Forty Days
With the Holy Spirit*, a sequel to my book *Holy
Fire*. I want to thank my editor Debbie Marrie for her
encouragement and her associate, Deborah Moss.

Since our retirement our son, Robert Tillman II
(whom we call TR), and Annette have given us two
wonderful grandsons—Tobias Robert and Timothy
Robert. Louise and I were not prepared for the
incredible and amazing pleasure that grandchildren
can give. It is our prayer that Toby and Timothy will
come to know the Lord Jesus while they are young
and will read this book as they get older. We want
them to experience a hunger for the Holy Spirit and
be filled with Him as Jesus promised.

—R. T. KENDALL

WWW.RTKENDALLMINISTRIES.COM

INTRODUCTION

I N MY BOOK *Holy Fire* I stated that there are twenty-one things every Christian should know about the Holy Spirit. But there is, to be sure, much more we need to know about Him. In this book I have done basically two things: (1) I have elaborated on these twenty-one principles, and (2) I have chosen nineteen more insights from the Bible about the Holy Spirit. This brings us to forty basic teachings about Him.

Why forty? Because *forty* is a number in the Bible that has had repeated significance. The flood in Noah's time came after forty days of rain (Gen. 7:17). Moses spent forty days on Mount Sinai (Exod. 24:18). Jesus fasted for forty days in the wilderness (Matt. 4:2). He ascended to heaven forty days after His resurrection (Acts 1:3). I therefore invite you to enter into a forty-day journey in pursuit of a greater measure of the Holy Spirit—not merely to learn more *about* Him, but to experience…*Him*. I wrote *Holy Fire* to make the reader hungry for the Holy Spirit. I have written this book in order that you might experience the immediate and direct witness of the Holy Spirit in greater measure than you have ever known. There is a difference between knowing *about* someone and knowing that person intimately.

The Holy Spirit welcomes you to enter into a close relationship with Him. I urge you to read this book prayerfully. One day at a time. Some might consider reading this on their knees. Yes, you *could* read the entire book in an hour or two. But you would miss the purpose of this book. I pray that this book will warm your heart, create a greater hunger in you, and lead to your being filled with the Holy Spirit. Jesus promised that those who hunger and thirst after righteousness shall be "filled" (Matt. 5:6). Paul prayed that we would be "filled to the measure of all the fullness of God" (Eph. 3:19); indeed, that we would be "filled with the Spirit" (Eph. 5:18).

Each day concludes with additional scriptures for further study as well as a prayer and space for you to journal what God is saying to you during this time. If you are doing this study as an e-book, use your personal journal or a notebook to record what God is speaking to you. May God bless you as you proceed.

Day 1

THE HOLY SPIRIT IS GOD

I BEGIN WITH THIS stunning truth because it is the most important thing that can be said about the Holy Spirit: that He is God. Fully God. The Holy Spirit is fully God as the Father is God and as Jesus the Son is God. We know that the Father is God; this is an assumption we accept uncritically—like saying God is God. And as Christians we equally believe and confess that Jesus is God. "In the beginning was the Word, and the Word was with God, and the Word was God" (John 1:1). The Word was made flesh (v. 14) and yet remained fully God. Jesus was (and is) God as though He were not man, and yet man as though He were not God. God Himself calls Jesus God, for He said to the Son, "Your throne, O God, will last for ever and ever" (Heb. 1:8). As John summed up his general epistle: Jesus Christ "is the true God" (1 John 5:20).

Therefore in the exact same way the Holy Spirit is truly, totally, and fully God—as God is God.

When Ananias lied to the Holy Spirit, he lied to

God. Peter said to him, "How is it that Satan has so filled your heart that you have lied to the Holy Spirit?...You have not lied to men but to God" (Acts 5:3–4). As a consequence Ananias (and afterward his wife, Sapphira) were immediately struck dead. The Holy Spirit was present in the earliest church at a very high level. They were in a "revival situation," which is something the church sadly is not experiencing at the moment. So when God is manifest as powerfully as He was at that time, it became dangerous to lie in His presence. Lying to the Holy Spirit was like tampering with high-voltage electricity with wet hands.

Paul also demonstrated the deity of the Holy Spirit when he said we are God's "temple." The temple is the place where God Himself dwells. "If anyone destroys God's temple, God will destroy him" (1 Cor. 3:16). Moreover, "Your body is a temple of the Holy Spirit, who is in you, whom you have received from God" (1 Cor. 6:19). This is another way of stating that the Holy Spirit is God. Paul also said, "The Lord is the Spirit" (2 Cor. 3:17).

We must therefore speak of the deity of the Holy Spirit—that He is God—because He is. We don't feel a need to speak of the deity of the Father, do we? It would seem redundant. And yet sometimes I think I would like to preach on the Godhood of God! The most neglected member of the Trinity these days is God the Father. There are more books written by

Christian authors on Jesus and on the Holy Spirit than on God the Father.

That said, never underestimate or take for granted the deity of the Holy Spirit. The Holy Spirit in you is God in you. You can *worship* the Holy Spirit; you can *pray* to the Holy Spirit; you can *sing* to the Holy Spirit. And yet there are some sincere Christians who are reluctant to pray or sing to the Holy Spirit. This is because of a faulty translation of John 16:13, which I will examine below. Such well-meaning Christians don't mind singing the first two verses of a well-known chorus that speaks of glorifying the Father and the Son, but when it comes to glorifying the Spirit, some are afraid to continue singing! As if the Spirit does not want to be worshipped and adored! Or as if the Father and the Son would not want this!

Such Christians feel uncomfortable singing about worshipping and adoring the Spirit because the King James Version translated John 16:13—referring to the Holy Spirit—"He shall not speak of himself," a verse that should be translated, "He will not speak *on His own*," as I show again later in this book. I actually sympathize with these people, however. I know where they are coming from. I used to have the same problem until I saw what the Greek literally said. And yet traditional church hymnals for many years have unashamedly included hymns with lyrics such as "Holy Spirit, Truth divine, dawn upon this soul of

mine,"[1] "Holy Ghost dispel our sadness,"[2] "Lord God,
the Holy Ghost, in this accepted hour, as on the day
of Pentecost, descend in all Thy power,"[3] or "Spirit of
God, descend upon my heart."[4] I love the words of
the following hymn:

> I worship Thee, O Holy Ghost,
> I love to worship Thee;
> My risen Lord for aye were lost
> But for Thy company.
>
> I worship Thee, O Holy Ghost,
> I love to worship Thee;
> With Thee each day is Pentecost,
> Each night Nativity.[5]

You could not address the Holy Spirit like that if
He were not God. Do not be afraid to talk directly
to the Holy Spirit. Or to sing to Him. There is no
jealousy or rivalry in the Trinity—the Father and Son
and Holy Spirit. The Father is happy and the Son is
happy when you address the Holy Spirit in prayer.
After all, the Spirit of God is God the Spirit. What is
more, the Trinity is not God the Father, God the Son,
and God the Holy Bible! Let this grip you.

Never forget, then: the Holy Spirit is God. Therefore
think about this: you may be *filled with God*. I want
to be passionate about *God*. Consider all the attributes of God. "The heavens declare the glory of God;

the skies proclaim the work of his hands" (Ps. 19:1). "When I consider your heavens, the work of your fingers, the moon and the stars, which you have set in place, what is man that you are mindful of him?" (Ps. 8:3–4). Ponder this: God your Creator and Redeemer is in you! You may be filled with Him. And this happens because you may be filled with the Holy Spirit—who is God.

For further study: Acts 5:1–13; 1 Corinthians 3:16–17; 1 Corinthians 6:19–20; 2 Corinthians 3:12–18

> *Come, Holy Spirit, come. Come as wind. Come as fire. That we might be filled, empowered, and cleansed. In Jesus's name, amen.*

_____

_____

_____

_____

_____

_____

Day 2

THE HOLY SPIRIT IS A PERSON

THE SECOND MOST important truth about the Holy Spirit is that He is a *person* in the Godhead. Jesus told us to baptize in "the name of the Father and of the Son and of the Holy Spirit" (Matt. 28:19). Paul closed one of his letters with this benediction: "May the grace of the Lord Jesus Christ, and the love of God, and the fellowship of the Holy Spirit be with you all" (2 Cor. 13:14). Peter began his first letter with the words "chosen according to the foreknowledge of God the Father, through the sanctifying work of the Spirit, for obedience to Jesus Christ and sprinkling by his blood" (1 Pet. 1:2).

In the early second century Tertullian (*c.* 160–*c.* 225) coined a phrase in Latin—*trinitas*, from which we get the word *trinity*. He also referred to the Father, Son, and Holy Spirit as *personas*—after which the church referred to the persons of the Godhead. The doctrine of the Trinity has been orthodox teaching for the Christian church for two thousand years. Don't try to figure out this teaching! Just believe it.

You don't try to figure out electricity; you just use it. The Trinity is given to us not to understand fully but fully to believe.

Therefore *Trinity* is a word that does not attempt to explain but merely to identify the persons in the Godhead. That said, the Father and the Son are each seen as "He." The Holy Spirit is also to be understood as "He." It is sad that the King James Version referred to the Holy Spirit as "it" in Romans 8:26—"the Spirit itself." Modern versions have corrected this, translating the Greek "the Spirit himself."

Jesus referred to the Holy Spirit as "he" (John 14:16; 16:8) and introduced Him as *allon parakletos*—the literal Greek translation being "another one [*allon*] who comes alongside [*parakletos*]." It is impossible to translate *parakletos* with one word, though it has been variously translated as "comforter," "advocate," "counselor," or "helper." All these describe exactly what Jesus was; He was a person who had come alongside the Twelve for some three years. The disciples knew Jesus at a natural level. They knew what He looked like; they knew the color of His eyes, the sound of His voice. He had been physically real to them for those three years; they saw Him, heard Him, and touched Him (1 John 1:1). Jesus was a real person.

Although invisible to us, the Holy Spirit likewise is a real person.

Therefore never think of the Holy Spirit as an "it,"

an "attitude," or an "influence." He is a *person* and has very definite ways. Call those ways peculiar, eccentric, or unique if you like; He has His *ways*. You may not like His ways. But get over it! He is the only Holy Spirit you have! He won't adjust to you; you must adjust to Him.

The Holy Spirit Himself spoke of ancient Israel as not knowing God's "ways" (Heb. 3:7–10). God was grieved because His own covenant people did not know His ways. They should have known them. But they didn't. God has His own "ways" and wants us to know them. And so too it is when it comes to the person of the Holy Spirit. He wants us to know His ways. As we will see below, the Spirit can be grieved, He can be quenched, and He can be blasphemed.

The Holy Spirit can also have *joy*. In Romans 14:17 Paul talked about "joy *in* the Holy Spirit" (emphasis added), whereas he referred to the "joy *of* the Holy Spirit" in 1 Thessalonians 1:6 (ESV, emphasis added). It is His own joy. This joy is not necessarily what *we* feel; it is what *He* feels. And yet sometimes He invites us to feel what He feels! It is called "gladness" in Acts 2:28 (ESV). That is exactly what I experienced years ago driving in my car, an event to which I will return later.

We need therefore to learn the difference between feeling happy because of circumstances and feeling the very "joy of the LORD" (Neh. 8:10). There is certainly nothing wrong with our feeling happy because things are working out for us. Indeed, there was "great joy in that city" when many who had been paralyzed were healed (Acts 8:7–8). The good news about Gentiles being converted made the disciples "very glad" (Acts 15:3). But the highest level of joy on this planet is when we are allowed to experience the very joy *of* the Spirit—feeling what He feels. Peter pointed out that his readers had not seen Jesus Himself but that they nonetheless experienced Him. "Though you have not seen him, you love him; and even though you do not see him now, you believe in him and are filled with an expressible and glorious joy" (1 Pet. 1:8). For when the person of the Holy Spirit lets us feel His joy, it is truly "inexpressible."

For further study: Nehemiah 8:10; John 14:16–21; 1 Corinthians 12:4–6; Ephesians 4:4–6; Hebrews 3:7–11; Jude 20–21

> *Holy Spirit, I welcome You afresh into my heart. Let me experience Your person and Your joy in ever-increasing measure. In Jesus's name, amen.*

_____

_____

_____

_____

Day 3

THE HOLY SPIRIT IS ETERNAL

WHO MADE GOD?" is the question we all cannot help but ask. I remember asking my mother this question when I was a child. I wasn't happy with her answer: "Nobody made God; He always was." The reason we aren't happy with the answer is that we prefer to think logically. Logic often seeks to remove the need for faith. What makes faith *faith* is that we simply accept that God always was and had no beginning. Faith is the assurance of things hoped for but without tangible evidence (Heb. 11:1). There are basically two worldviews when it comes to faith: (1) the secular atheist view: "I will believe it when I see it," or seeing is believing; and (2) the biblical view: believing God without seeing the proof. The Bible makes no attempt to prove the existence of God. The word of God begins, simply, "In the beginning God created the heavens and the earth" (Gen. 1:1).

So it is with the eternal existence of God. I choose to believe the Bible—the infallible word of God. I happen to believe totally that the Bible is true. This is because of the inner testimony of the Holy Spirit. The Holy Spirit has persuaded me that the Bible is true. The Bible says that God is eternal: "The eternal God is your refuge, and underneath are the everlasting arms" (Deut. 33:27). The apostle John had a vision of the living creatures in heaven that worship God day and night:

> Holy, holy, holy is the Lord God Almighty, who was, and is, and is to come.
>
> —REVELATION 4:8

And so the Holy Spirit—like the Father and the Son—is eternal. This means none of the persons of the Trinity had a beginning. There is a subtle but important distinction between eternal and everlasting. *Eternal* means no beginning as well as no end. *Everlasting* means no end. For example, the angels are everlasting but not eternal; they had a beginning because they were created. Both the Father and the Son are eternal—no beginning, no end. The Word—Jesus—was in the beginning with God (John 1:2). Paul wrote, "For by him all things were created: things in heaven and on earth, visible and invisible, whether thrones or powers or rulers or authorities; all things were created by him and for him. He is before all things, and in him all things hold together" (Col. 1:16–17).

Like the Father and the Son, then, the Holy Spirit is not only everlasting but also eternal; He had no beginning—because He is God. "How much more, then, will the blood of Christ, who through *the eternal Spirit* offered himself unblemished to God, cleanse our consciences from acts that lead to death, so that we may serve the living God!" (Heb. 9:14, emphasis added). The Father, the Son, and the Spirit existed in eternity before God chose to create the heavens and the earth (Gen. 1:1). "Before the mountains were born or you brought forth the whole world, from everlasting to everlasting you are God" (Ps. 90:2). As I stated above, God the Father is eternal, and so is the Holy Spirit. When Paul said that in the fullness of time God "sent his Son" (Gal. 4:4), it is because the Father already had a Son. Jesus Christ is the eternal Son. He was the Word until the moment He became "flesh" (John 1:14). After then He could be called the God-man. The Lord Jesus Christ did not begin in Bethlehem but at His conception in Nazareth the moment the Word entered the womb of the Virgin Mary.

The Holy Spirit is equally eternal with the Father and the Word. This is the same Holy Spirit that is mentioned many times in the Old Testament; indeed, the same eternal person Jesus talked about and introduced to His disciples—not that the Twelve grasped that the Holy Spirit was eternal when He was first introduced to them. So much of what Jesus taught was not understood for a good while. They did not even know—at the time—that Jesus was eternal! This was a truth that they took on board little by little after Jesus ascended to heaven.

As we will see again below, Jesus said that the Holy Spirit spoke through David in Psalm 110:1 (Matt. 22:43). It was the testimony of the early church that God spoke "by the Holy Spirit through the mouth of your servant, our father David" (Acts 4:25). Indeed, the Holy Spirit had a role in Creation and was the Author of all Scripture.

In a word: the Holy Spirit is eternal just like the Father and the Son.

For further study: Genesis 1:1–3; Psalm 90; 139; John 1:1–14; 1 Corinthians 2:10–16

> *Eternal Spirit, I am so honored to know You live in me. To think You have always been and always will be overwhelms me. I worship You and ask You to rule my whole life. In Jesus's name, amen.*

_____

_____

_____

_____

Day 4

THE HOLY SPIRIT WAS
INVOLVED IN CREATION

WHEN I WAS first ordained to the ministry in Ashland, Kentucky, in 1964, I was publicly questioned by one of my old mentors, Dr. N. B. Magruder. He wanted me to demonstrate to the congregation that I was worthy to be ordained, so he asked me certain theological questions. I had no idea what was coming. One of the questions referred to the eternality of the Holy Spirit. Dr. Magruder asked me to explain the Holy Spirit in the Old Testament. I wasn't prepared for that question. However, I began by referring to the role of the Holy Spirit in Creation, after which I told all I could think of regarding this subject. I barely managed, but that event caused me to think more deeply regarding the teaching of the Holy Spirit in the Old Testament.

As we will see further below, there are many references to the Holy Spirit in the Old Testament, some of which I will elaborate on later in this book. He was, in fact, present and active the whole time—from

Creation on! For example, Pharaoh discerned that the Spirit of God was in Joseph (Gen. 41:38). Bezalel was "filled with the Spirit of God" (Exod. 31:3). The "Spirit of the LORD" was upon Othniel (Judg. 3:9–10), Gideon (Judg. 6:34), Jephthah (Judg. 11:29), Saul (1 Sam. 10:10), and David (1 Sam. 16:13). The Holy Spirit lay behind the ministry of Elijah (1 Kings 18:12; 2 Kings 2:16). The Spirit of God came upon Azariah (2 Chron. 15:1) and Zechariah (2 Chron. 24:20). The references to the Holy Spirit go on and on. One of the greatest of all is this: "Not by might, nor by power, but by my Spirit, saith the LORD of hosts" (Zech. 4:6, KJV).

But back to Creation. God the Father was the primary agent in initiating the act of Creation. However, the Son and the Holy Spirit were also active. The Son is often described as the one "through" whom Creation came about. "Through him all things were made; without him nothing was made that has been made" (John 1:3). Paul said that there is "one Lord, Jesus Christ, through whom all things came and through whom we live" (1 Cor. 8:6). The Son is the one "through whom he [God] made the universe" (Heb. 1:2). In the same way the Holy Spirit was at work in Creation. The Holy Spirit is generally pictured as completing, filling, and giving life to God's creation.

"The Spirit of God was hovering over the waters" (Gen. 1:2), indicating a persevering, sustaining, and governing function. "The Spirit of God has made me; the breath of the Almighty gives me life" (Job 33:4). The word *Spirit* in the Old Testament is from the Hebrew word *ruach*, which means "wind," "breath," or "spirit." The wind of God—or breath of God—could be a figurative way of referring to the Holy Spirit's activity in Creation. So the psalmist, in speaking of the great activity of creatures on the earth and in the sea, says, "When you send forth Your Spirit, they are created" (Ps. 104:30, NKJV).

As we just saw, Jesus, the second person of the Trinity, is depicted as Creator. "For by him all things were created: things in heaven and on earth, visible and invisible, whether thrones or powers or rulers or authorities; all things were created by him and for him. He is before all things, and in him all things hold together" (Col. 1:16–17). Some of these lines could equally describe the Holy Spirit—for example, that He is before all things.

The point is, we must never forget that the Holy Spirit had a hand in Creation, just as Jesus did.

For further study: Genesis 1:1–3; Psalm 104:24–30; 136:5–9; Revelation 4:8–11

> *Glorious Holy Spirit, when I consider that You had a role in Creation, it means You also had a role in making me! And now You dwell in me! Thank You for this truth. Do*

make me ever-increasingly grateful to You
for being my Creator. In Jesus's name, amen.

_____

_____

_____

_____

_____

_____

_____

_____

_____

_____

_____

Day 5

THE HOLY SPIRIT
GIVES WARNINGS

IN NOAH'S DAY God said, "My Spirit will not contend with man forever" (Gen. 6:3). I grew up on the King James Version, which says, "My Spirit shall not always strive with man." The implication is that there is a limit to God's patience with humankind. He is "slow to anger," yes (Exod. 34:6). But when He finally stops warning sinful people and manifests His judgment, the consequences can be pretty horrible.

I vividly recall evangelists coming to my old church in Ashland, Kentucky, back in the 1940s and 1950s. They would quote this Old Testament verse frequently—Genesis 6:3—when warning people of God's impending judgment. Invitational hymns like "Almost Persuaded" and "Pass Me Not, O Gentle Savior" frequently followed sermons that warned of the danger of people postponing getting right with God. It was always stressed, "Now is the time of God's favor, now is the day of salvation" (2 Cor. 6:2).

There is no promise of tomorrow. God might say to the person who thinks he has "many years" left: "You fool! This very night your life will be demanded from you" (Luke 12:20). This gives you a hint of my earliest background.

It is out of the kindness of God that He gives warnings. "Note then the kindness and the severity of God," said Paul (Rom. 11:22, ESV). And yet God gives warnings only when there is still hope. Such a warning is an example of His kindness. Jonah marched into Nineveh with the warning: "Forty more days and Nineveh will be overturned" (Jon. 3:4). There was no explicit promise of mercy if they repented, but the Ninevites "believed God" and "declared a fast, and all of them, from the greatest to the least, put on sackcloth" (v. 5). The consequence of their repentance was: "When God saw what they did and how they turned from their evil ways, he had compassion and did not bring upon them the destruction he had threatened" (v. 10).

As I said, Jonah's message did not offer any hope to the people of Nineveh. For all I know, this absence of a promise of mercy may have been what shook them rigid. You may ask: since Jonah clearly said that Nineveh *would be overthrown* in forty days—with no apparent hope—how was it possible that God did not keep His word but had mercy upon them? The answer is this: God never warns when there is no hope. For example, there is no indication that God ever warned Sodom and Gomorrah for their wickedness. He just punished them instead. So if God sends warning, take it with both hands! Be glad. Heed the warning.

When I was a teenager, an aged visiting evangelist announced, "Someone here is getting their last call." He refused to close the service and handed it over to the pastor. The pastor refused to end the service and sat down. The people slowly got up out of their seats and went home. The next day as I finished my paper route (I delivered the *Ashland Daily Independent* to 110 homes in the neighborhood), my mother said, "Did you hear about Sandy*?" "No," I replied. "What do you mean?" Only moments before, one of my friends was suddenly killed by a car out of control as she walked home from school. She was in the congregation—scoffing at the preacher's sermon—the day before when the evangelist said, "Someone here is getting their last call." The effect of that event upon me was incalculable.

"It is of the LORD's mercies that we are not consumed" (Lam. 3:22, KJV). In Jonathan Edwards's unforgettable sermon "Sinners in the Hands of an Angry God" (July 8, 1741) he said, "It is by the very mercy of God you are not in hell right now."[1] When he finished, people were seen holding on to pews in the

---

* Not her real name

church—and also outside holding on to tree trunks—to keep from falling into hell. It was one of those rare moments when God came down in unusual power. God's mercy is often demonstrated by His warning us. "So, as the Holy Spirit says: 'Today, if you hear his voice, do not harden your hearts as you did in the rebellion, during the time of testing in the desert'" (Heb. 3:7–8). The eventual result was that God swore in His wrath, "They shall never enter my rest" (v. 11).

The Bible says basically two things about God: He is merciful and He is just. By merciful it means He does not want to punish us; by just it means He must punish us. Is there a way whereby He can be merciful and just at the same time? Yes. He sent His Son into the world to die on a cross—and punished Jesus for *our* sins. That was His justice. This way He does not have to punish those who trust Jesus's blood for salvation. That is His mercy.

Do you know for sure that if you died today you would go to heaven? Transfer your trust in your good works to Jesus's death on the cross, and you will be saved. But don't wait. "My Spirit will not always strive with man." How gracious are the warnings of the Holy Spirit.

For further study: Genesis 4:6–7; 18:25; Matthew 3:7–10; Luke 12:13–21

O gracious Holy Spirit, thank You for Your warnings. I know You warn us because we are loved. Grant us grace to wake up before it is too late. In Jesus's name, amen.

_____

_____

_____

_____

_____

_____

_____

_____

_____

_____

_____

Day 6

THE HOLY SPIRIT VINDICATES

M Y FAVORITE OLD Testament story is that of Joseph. He was given dreams that indicated his eleven brothers would one day bow down to him. His mistake was telling the dreams to his brothers! They decided to kill him but changed their minds and sold Joseph to the Ishmaelites—never expecting to see him again. But God was with Joseph. He was sold to an Egyptian officer named Potiphar and won favor. During this time he refused Potiphar's wife's flirtations, so she accused him of trying to rape her. He was put in prison. While there he interpreted the dream of Pharaoh's cupbearer. Years later Pharaoh had a dream that no one could interpret. The cupbearer remembered Joseph, who was instantly released from prison in order to interpret Pharaoh's dream. When Pharaoh heard the interpretation, he said, "Can we find a man like this, in whom is the Spirit of God?" (Gen. 41:38, ESV), this being one of grandest references to the Holy Spirit in the Old Testament. Joseph by the help of the Holy Spirit interpreted Pharaoh's dream, and Joseph's own dreams were soon fulfilled.

Joseph was made prime minister of Egypt. Sometime after that his eleven brothers came to buy food in Egypt and had to go to the prime minister—bowing to him, having no idea he was their brother. It was then that Joseph's dreams were perfectly fulfilled. The Holy Spirit brought vindication to Joseph.

You could say either that *Joseph* was vindicated or the *truth of his dreams* was vindicated. When it comes to vindication—being proved right, especially when misunderstood or falsely accused—remember two things. First, God only vindicates honesty and integrity and those on the side of truth and justice. Therefore falsely accused or misunderstood people deserve vindication only when truth and justice are on their side. So if you deserve vindication, you will get it—sooner or later. The psalmist wrote, "Delight yourself in the LORD and he will give you the desires of your heart. Commit your way to the LORD; trust in him and he will do this: he will make your righteousness shine like the dawn, the justice of your cause like the noonday sun' (Ps. 37:4–6). Second, vindication is what God does best. Do not deprive Him of doing what He is an expert on. Don't elbow in on His territory. If you do, you will only delay the process. But if you will leave matters to God to order and provide, He will vindicate in a matter you never dreamed possible. But if the truth is not at stake, don't expect vindication.

"It is mine to avenge; I will repay," says the Lord

(Deut. 32:35; Rom. 12:19). This is the Holy Spirit's prerogative. But He may not do it today or tomorrow! Joseph waited some twenty-two years before his dreams were vindicated. In my book *Total Forgiveness* I point out that Joseph's vindication was delayed until *he got right in himself* and totally forgave his brothers for what they did.

Are you waiting for vindication? I sympathize with you. I know what it is to be falsely accused, set aside, misunderstood, and maligned. I have had this from my own family—from a godly father and grandmother. They were as sincere as they could be. They felt I had broken with God. I waited a long, long time before my dad said to me, "Son, I am proud of you. You were right; I was wrong." As for my grandmother, she went to heaven fully believing I had missed the mark. In heaven the truth will be vindicated. It is not personal. It seems personal when we are falsely accused. It hurts. But if it is the *truth* we are standing for, you can count on this—God will get involved! He may take time. It may be *we* need sorting out while we wait. Do you need sorting out? Do you need to forgive someone who has been hurtful? Joseph had a lot of sorting out to do before he could be trusted with greatness.

You may even get vindication from someone whose opinion doesn't particularly matter to you. I don't think Pharaoh's vindicating and exalting Joseph meant all that much to Joseph. Joseph's heart was back in Canaan—where his brothers lived. Being cleared before them was more important than being made prime minister of Egypt. And perhaps that is another reason Joseph could be trusted with such a lofty position; it didn't matter to him all that much!

When it comes to having your name cleared, let the Holy Spirit do it! He does it best. He will do it in a manner that is dazzling—in a way you could have never dreamed. But don't rush the Holy Spirit. Let Him do His own work in His time, and you will be so glad you did not interfere.

For further study: Genesis 41:16; Matthew 23:12; 1 Corinthians 4:4–5; 1 Peter 5:6–10

> *Holy Spirit, please forgive me for my impatience in trying to get vindication. I am sorry. I turn everything over to You, knowing You will reveal the truth in Your own time. In Jesus's name, amen.*

_____

_____

_____

_____

_____

Day 7

THE HOLY SPIRIT GIVES TALENT

W E NOW EMBARK upon a teaching called "common grace"—God's goodness to everybody whether they are saved or lost. God causes His sun to shine and rain to fall on the just and unjust (Matt. 5:45). It is God's *special grace in nature.* We call it "common" not because it is ordinary but because it is given commonly to all people— saved, lost, young, old, Americans, Brits, Indians, Chinese, rich, poor, red, yellow, black, or white. When I refer to special grace in nature, I refer to one's *natural* ability, talent, intellect, or gift. The Spirit of God is the explanation. Though it is our "natural" ability or talent on display, it is nonetheless the Spirit of God who is responsible for our IQ; our ability to play an instrument, practice medicine, or drive a truck; and whether we are cerebral, gifted in athletics, able to work with a computer, or to teach. Such people, as I said, may or may not be saved. I have no idea whether Sergei Rachmaninoff was a Christian, but I love to hear his music. Albert Einstein had one of the greatest intellects in the twentieth century, but there is no evidence he was a Christian. Sometimes highly gifted people become Christians—such as St. Augustine, John Calvin, or Jonathan Edwards—and the church is all the better for it. But most of us are ordinary (1 Cor. 1:26).

The teaching of common grace emerges early in the Old Testament. A man named Bezalel was gifted with a special skill. It pertained to "ability and knowledge in all kinds of crafts—to make artistic designs for work in gold, silver and bronze, to cut and set stones, to work in wood, and to engage in all kinds of craftsmanship" (Exod. 31:3–5). And where did this talent come from? "The Lord said to Moses, 'See, I have chosen Bezalel son of Uri…and I have *filled him with the Spirit of God*, with skill, ability and knowledge" (vv. 1–3, emphasis added).

Have you ever heard of Jubal? "He was the father of all who play the harp and flute" (Gen. 4:21). What do you know about Tubal-Cain? He "forged all kinds of tools out of bronze and iron" (v. 22). These were talents that have their origin in the Spirit of God.

When Solomon began to build the temple, he turned to Hiram and said: "Give orders that cedars of Lebanon be cut for me…You know that we have no one so skilled in felling timber as the Sidonians" (1 Kings 5:6). "The craftsmen of Solomon and Hiram and the men of Gebal cut and prepared the timber and stone for the building of the temple" (v. 18). In other words, in order to build the temple, Solomon went outside Israel to get some of the work done. He would be thankful that there are people in the world with particular gifts and talents. The explanation: the Spirit of God.

Common grace is what keeps the world from being topsy-turvy. Thank God for traffic lights, for hospitals, for firemen, for policemen, for doctors and nurses.

You have a talent that God gave you. It is not necessarily because you are a Christian. You received this talent from your parents and the influences of your environment, peer relationships, and education. Thank God for these. "For who makes you different from anyone else? What do you have that you did not receive? And if you did receive it, why do you boast as though you did not?" (1 Cor. 4:7). Have you thanked God for His goodness to you at the natural level? Did you know that it is been proven by a group of psychologists that thankful people live longer?[1]

"By the grace of God I am what I am" (1 Cor. 15:10). You have the blessed Spirit of God to thank for *everything good* in your life. Sometimes spiritual gifts overlap with what may be called motivational gifts. Gifted people in the church are given positions and responsibilities not necessarily because they are more spiritual but, simply, more able. Such ability is often to be derived from common grace—whether serving, teaching, encouraging, or leadership (Rom. 12:7–8). God uses one's natural ability in the church to advance His kingdom. Charles Spurgeon used to say that if God calls you to preach, He will give you "a pair of lungs"—especially in days when there were no public address systems![2]

We should pray that God would raise up more men and women in the church with great natural talent. It is a pity when able people offer their gifts to the world when, in fact, they came from the Spirit of God.

For further study: Psalm 45:1–6; Matthew 5:43–45; 1 Corinthians 4:6–7; James 1:17

> *Gracious Holy Spirit, teach me how great God is! Thank You for all the things you give us because You love Your creation— flowers, food, change of seasons, people You put in our path, our natural ability and grace in us we so easily take for granted. In Jesus's name, amen.*

Day 8

THE HOLY SPIRIT OVERRULES

MY FAMILY AND I moved to Oxford, England, in 1973 in order for me to do my doctor of philosophy degree. I had my heart set on writing a thesis on the theology of the puritan John Owen (1616–1683). On a pivotal occasion my supervisors Dr. B. R. White and Dr. J. I. Packer had lunch with me to give me news I did not want to hear. "Shall you tell him or should I?" Dr. White said to Dr. Packer. They brought their verdict that I should "minimize my liabilities"—that I must give up my plans to do a thesis on John Owen but take a different line. My supervisors had overruled my plans. I was devastated. I went home with a migraine headache. But, in fact, their advice was the best thing that happened to me at Oxford. I eventually came to see it as God kindly overruling my plans.

To overrule means to disallow by exercising one's superior authority. Have you lived long enough to appreciate God overruling in your life? The first time it is written that the Spirit of God overruled in the life of Israel was when the false prophet Balaam attempted to prophesy against Israel. Balak king of Moab asked Balaam to curse Israel because "those you bless are blessed and those you curse are cursed" (Num. 22:6). But when Balaam attempted to prophesy, "the Spirit of God came upon him," and he uttered a prophecy that positively blessed Israel (Num. 24:2–9). Think of that! The Spirit of God overruled the intentions of a false prophet. For generations this event would be looked back upon with great fondness by Israel. Moses observed that Balak, Israel's enemy, hired Balaam to curse Israel, but "the LORD your God would not listen to Balaam but turned the curse into a blessing for you, because the LORD your God loves you" (Deut. 23:5; see also Josh. 24:10; Neh. 13:2).

The history of Israel is replete with instances when God overruled in the life of Israel because He loved Israel. God overruled the plans of Pharaoh to keep the Israelites in bondage. He sent plagues upon Egypt and enabled the Israelites to cross the Red Sea, and then He destroyed the Egyptians who tried again to defeat Israel (Exod. 14:29–31). God overruled the plans of Sennacherib to destroy Israel when He sent an angel to put 185,000 men to death (2 Kings 19:35).

The history of Israel is also full of accounts when God overruled for the sake of individual servants. When Korah challenged Moses's authority, God overruled and destroyed Korah and his rebellious followers (Num. 16:31–35). King Nebuchadnezzar was determined to annihilate Shadrach, Meshach, and Abednego by casting them into a burning furnace. God overruled. The Son of God joined these three men—which amazed the king when he saw *four* men walking in the blazing furnace. The fire had not harmed them, "nor was a hair of their heads singed" (Dan. 3:27). After that the administrators of King Darius were motivated by jealousy toward Daniel. They manipulated the king into signing a decree that put Daniel into a lions' den. God overruled and "shut the mouths of the lions" (Dan. 6:22).

The high priest arrested the apostles of Jesus and put them in the public jail. But God overruled. "During the night an angel of the Lord opened the doors of the jail and brought them out" (Acts 5:19). Peter was extremely biased toward Gentiles. He piously said to God, "I have never eaten anything impure or unclean." God said, "Do not call anything impure that God has made clean" (Acts 10:14–15). God overruled. Peter learned a lesson: "I now realize how true it is that God does not show favoritism" (v. 34).

If it were not for the overruling grace of God, none of us would be preserved, taught new lessons—or even saved. Saul of Tarsus was on his way to kill Christians in Damascus. God overruled. Suddenly a light from heaven flashed around him, and he fell to the ground. The result was that he prayed, "What shall I do, Lord?" (Acts 22:6–10). Paul wrote to the Ephesians, noting that "we all once lived in the passions of our flesh, carrying out the desires of the body and the mind, and were by nature children of wrath, like the rest of mankind. *But God*, being rich in mercy…made us alive…and raised us up with him" (Eph. 2:3–6, esv). But God.

The gracious Holy Spirit overrules in our lives all the time. I predict that when we get to heaven we will ask God to let us see countless DVDs of how angels intervened and overruled in our lives—when we were not conscious of all that was going on. Thank God for the Holy Spirit's overruling grace.

For further study: Psalm 124; Daniel 6:3–24; Acts 9:1–15; Ephesians 2:1–9

> *Blessed Holy Spirit, thank You for the ways You have overruled again and again in my life. I blush to think about it. Just make me thankful for Your exceeding kindnesses. In Jesus's name, amen.*

_____

_____

_____

_____

Day 9

THE HOLY SPIRIT
TRANSFERS ANOINTING

I HAVE SAID MANY times that I would rather have a greater anointing than anything. I suppose that is a God-honoring request, but I am not so sure. I want it so much that I cannot tell whether this desire is natural or spiritual. The anointing is the power of the Holy Spirit that makes our gift function with ease. When I live within my anointing, my gift works without effort, but the moment I go outside my anointing, I find myself struggling.

God does not want us to struggle. He wants us to cast our anxiety on Him (1 Pet. 5:7). But at least twice in his life Moses struggled. First, he was over-whelmed by people coming to him in droves to get his verdict on civil matters among the children of Israel. His wise father-in-law, Jethro, saw all that Moses was doing for the people and said to him, "Why do you alone sit as judge, while all these people stand around you from morning till evening? . . . What you are doing is not good. You and these people who come to you will only wear yourselves out. The work is too heavy for you; you cannot handle it alone" (Exod. 18:14–18). Jethro then advised Moses to designate authority to others—appointing capable men as officials over thousands, hundreds, fifties, and tens—letting them handle the simple cases and Moses the more difficult (vv. 19–26).

The second occasion was when the people complained about the food—pining for what they ate in Egypt and lamenting that they now "never see anything but this manna!" (Num. 11:6). Moses brought this to the Lord and told Him that he could not bear the burden of their constant complaining. Moses was then instructed to choose seventy elders. God assured Moses that He would lighten his load: "I will take of the Spirit that is on you and put the Spirit on [the seventy]. They will help you carry the burden of the people so that you will not have to carry it alone" (v. 17). After that the Lord came down in a cloud and spoke with Moses. God "took of the Spirit that was on him and put the Spirit on the seventy elders. When the Spirit rested on them, they prophesied, but they did not do so again" (v. 25). However, two of them who had remained in the camp prophesied, and Joshua was upset. "Stop them!" he said to Moses. "Are you jealous for my sake?" he asked Joshua. "I wish that all the LORD's people were prophets and that the LORD would put his Spirit on them!" (vv. 28–29).

Why would Moses want everybody to prophesy and all to have the Spirit on them? Because when one person is in leadership and sees people struggle with their maladies, he realizes he needs all the help he can get! Joshua had not yet inherited Moses's mantle and wrongly assumed that Moses wanted to be the head and center of everything. How wrong Joshua was. The transfer of anointing to others lightens the load of the one with whom the buck stops. When all the people have the Spirit on them, it will mean that the work of God functions with ease—and with no rival spirit in control.

We learn from this how God can take from our anointing and pass it on to others. We are not told that Moses laid hands on the seventy elders. The impression is given that God merely did it by Himself—taking from Moses's anointing and passing it on without Moses losing any measure of the Spirit in the process. This is the wonderful thing about Christian ministry; what we give away we keep.

Nothing would be more thrilling than God taking from one's ministry and passing it on to others. I have longed for the day that not only would my anointing change lives and increase their measure of the Holy Spirit but also even heal people's bodies under my preaching. But if we want to keep the Holy Spirit to ourselves, it is unlikely that God will use us much.

We also learn from this account that God does not

want us to bear a heavy load. He knows how much we can bear and will step in—never too late, never too early, but always just on time.

For further study: Exodus 18:9–26; Numbers 11:4–30; 1 Corinthians 14:1–6; Revelation 10:8–11

Sovereign Spirit of God, I ask You to grant me an ever-increasing anointing and that it might be transferred to many people for Your honor and glory. In Jesus's name, amen.

_____

_____

_____

_____

_____

_____

_____

_____

_____

Day 10

THE HOLY SPIRIT EMPOWERS FOR LEADERSHIP

O NE OF THE questions I will ask the Lord when we get to heaven is, "Why did You not raise up a successor to Joshua? You made Joshua successor to Moses but provided no successor to Joshua." It is a mystery. Whatever the reason, Joshua was not succeeded by one man but by judges, or leaders sometimes called deliverers, during the time between Joshua and Samuel. Four of these men have in common that the "Spirit of the LORD came upon him" (Othniel, Judges 3:10; Gideon, Judges 6:34; Jephthah, Judges 11:29; and Samson, Judges 14:6, 19, 15:14). We know little about Othniel, but we know that in the case of the other three, each was characterized by a glaring weakness. Gideon was probably the best of the lot, but his stature diminished when toward the end of his life he requested that the people give him an earring. Gideon made the gold earrings into a gold ephod, which he placed in Ophrah, his town. "All Israel prostituted themselves by worshiping it there, and it became a snare to Gideon and his family" (Judg. 8:27).

John Calvin said that "in every saint there is something reprehensible." He said this in his commentary on Jephthah, who delivered Israel in an amazing victory over the Ammonites but would always be known for his foolish vow. Jephthah vowed to God that if He delivered Israel in this major battle, he would sacrifice anyone who "comes out of the door of my house" (Judg. 11:31). But who should it be but his own daughter! (vv. 34–35). In the case of Samson, sometimes called the strongest man who ever lived, he had a fatal weakness—a weakness for women. This weakness led to his downfall. He fell for Delilah, but she accused him of not loving her because he would not reveal his secret to her. He surely knew she was a bad person, but his desire for her overruled common sense. He revealed his secret—he had never had a haircut. When he slept, she cut off his hair, and his strength immediately left him. He became as weak as any man. The Philistines seized him, gouged out his eyes, and bound him with shackles. But when his hair began to grow, his strength returned. He brought down the temple, and all the people in it, getting vengeance upon them. He killed many more when he died than while he lived (Judg. 16:30).

Leaders need more than empowerment. They need wisdom. Young Solomon had the presence of mind to ask God for wisdom: "Give your servant a discerning heart to govern your people and to distinguish between right and wrong" (1 Kings 3:9). Solomon's wisdom was legendary in his own day and ever after. The Spirit of God gave power for leadership to these judges, but that was all. Why didn't the Holy Spirit lead them to cleansing as well as power for leadership? You tell me. The Book of Judges is summed up in the very last verse: "In those days Israel had no king; everyone did as he saw fit" (Judg. 21:15); or, in other words, "Everyone did what was right in his own eyes" (ESV).

There is a melancholy debate in some circles—which is more important, character or gifting? You would have thought that Christian leaders would have no difficulty answering a question like this, but—believe it or not—there are a lot of them who actually say that gifting is more important than character. In other words, if a person shows great leadership and oratory, and is able to prophesy or do miracles, a person's personal and private life does not matter. Really? No wonder the sexual immorality among Christian leaders nowadays!

The Holy Spirit is able to empower, yes. And He empowers for leadership. True. But power is not enough. We need purity too.

I fear that too many leaders want power only. Some of them have a vast following. Great charisma.

But that's about it. I don't mean to be unfair, but Paul did say that in the last days people would easily be deceived. "For the time will come when men will not put up with sound doctrine. Instead, to suit their own desires, they will gather around them a great number of teachers to say what their itching ears want to hear. They will turn their ears away from the truth, and turn aside to myths" (2 Tim. 4:3–4). Jesus said, "Many will say to me on that day, 'Lord, Lord, did we not prophesy in your name, and in your name drive out demons and perform many miracles? Then I will tell you plainly, 'I never knew you'" (Matt. 7:22–23).

Even though the Spirit of God still comes on some people—and they make a great show and wow the people—we should never follow them as our models, much less our mentors.

These things said, it may be surprise you that Gideon, Jephthah, and Samson all earned a place in the great faith chapter of the Bible—Hebrews 11. (See verse 32.) It goes to show that God is merciful. He knows our frame, remembering that we are dust (Ps. 103:14).

For further study: Matthew 7:15–27; Romans 11:29; 1 Timothy 4:1–5; 2 Timothy 4:1–5

> *O Holy Spirit, grant me the discernment to recognize the absence of wisdom and purity in leaders today. Let me not be*

among those who have itching ears and are not totally interested in the truth. In Jesus's name, amen.

_____

_____

_____

_____

_____

_____

_____

_____

_____

_____

_____

_____

Day 11

THE HOLY SPIRIT EMPOWERS FOR PROPHECY

O UR DEVOTIONAL TODAY is very similar to the previous one. The manner in which the Spirit of the Lord was referred to in the Book of Judges is repeated in 1 Samuel; that is, when it comes to King Saul.

We begin with Samuel—the first major prophet since Moses—and Israel's request for a king. Samuel pleaded with them not to ask for a king, but he gave into them. From that moment Samuel did his best to find them a king. Saul, the son of Kish, from the tribe of Benjamin was chosen. Samuel prophesied to Saul, "The Spirit of the LORD will come upon you in power, and you will prophesy...and you will be changed into a different person" (1 Sam. 10:6). Shortly after that "the Spirit of God came upon him in power," and he began prophesying (v. 10). Some of those who knew him asked, "What is this that has happened to the son of Kish? Is Saul among the prophets?" (v. 11).

King Saul had a brilliant beginning. He was given

great authority. On one occasion "the Spirit of God came upon him in power, and he burned with anger. He took a pair of oxen, cut them into pieces, and sent the pieces by messengers throughout Israel, proclaiming, 'This is what will be done to the oxen of anyone who does not follow Saul and Samuel.' Then the terror of the LORD fell on the people, and they turned out as one man" (1 Sam. 11:6–7).

But in a short period of time Saul became "yesterday's man," as I put it in my book *The Anointing: Yesterday, Today, Tomorrow.* What went wrong? In a word, he took himself too seriously. Dr. Martyn Lloyd-Jones used to say to me, "The worst thing that can happen to a man is to succeed before he is ready." That was Saul. The turning point came when Saul would not wait for Samuel to offer the burnt offerings. So Saul said, "Bring me the burnt offering and the fellowship offerings." Saul then offered up the burnt offering—knowingly going against Scripture that stipulates only the priest called of God can do that. Saul did it anyway. Samuel then showed up and said to King Saul, "You acted foolishly." Furthermore, "Your kingdom will not endure; the LORD has sought out a man after his own heart" (1 Sam. 13:9–14).

Things were never the same again—for Saul or for Israel. Saul was rejected by God. The people did not know this; only Samuel knew it. In the meantime Samuel anointed young David (1 Sam. 16:13)—the man after God's own heart. David killed Goliath, making Saul insanely jealous. Moreover, "Saul was afraid of David, because the LORD was with David but had left Saul" (1 Sam. 18:12).

David had to go into hiding because of Saul's jealousy and dogged determination to kill him. Saul was more concerned about the threat of David than he was the Philistines—the enemy of Israel. Saul was totally committed in his mind and heart to get rid of David. No persuading would change him, whether from his son Jonathan or daughter Michal.

And now we examine a surprising, truly extraordinary occurrence. On one of his expeditions to find David and kill him, King Saul began to prophesy. His prophetic gift had not left him. Strange as it may seem, "the Spirit of God came even upon him, and he walked along prophesying until he came to Naioth. He stripped of his robes and also prophesied in Samuel's presence. He lay that way all that day and night. This is why people say, 'Is Saul also among the prophets?'" (1 Sam. 19:23–24).

Think about this. Put these two things together: Saul prophesying and simultaneously planning to kill David. However can the two coincide? However could the *Spirit of God* come upon a man with such a wicked goal? If the Spirit of God fell on David when being anointed by Samuel, how could the same Spirit of God fall on the man whose sole obsession was to kill the man after God's own heart?

You tell me. This goes to show some of the mysteries that surround the manifestations of the Holy Spirit. What is more, Saul prophesied in the presence of Samuel, who had just anointed David to be king. Why didn't Samuel say something to Saul? He apparently remained silent.

There are some things that happen in the work of the Lord you cannot figure out. The Bible itself doesn't try to explain some things. We are left to "work out" our salvation with fear and trembling (Phil. 2:12). I take "work out" to mean to sort out some dilemmas as best and honestly as you know how. God does not spoon-feed us with every detail we would gladly welcome. He apparently expects us to grow up and come to conclusions that give us peace of mind.

There is one verse that gives me a sense of sanity on this kind of issue: "God's gifts and his call are irrevocable ['without repentance,' KJV]" (Rom. 11:29). Like it or not, God gives gifts—and lets us keep them—regardless of our character or conduct. This is why some people think that gifting has priority over character. I don't agree. I do not believe it is glorifying to God to live private lives that ignore holy living even though our gift may flourish.

What say you?

For further study: Acts 21:10–14; Philippians 2:12–16;
1 Thessalonians 4:3–7; Hebrews 12:15–17

> *Dear Holy Spirit, there is so much in Your word that I do not understand. Please give me grace to leave things with You but, at the same time, walk in a manner that brings great honor and glory to Your name. In Jesus's name, amen.*

_____

_____

_____

_____

_____

_____

_____

_____

_____

Day 12

THE HOLY SPIRIT PREPARES
US FOR SERVICE

WHEN SAMUEL POURED oil upon young David, anointing him to be the next king, the Spirit of the Lord came upon him in power (1 Sam. 16:13). But there is one thing that did not happen, namely, a further prophetic word from Samuel. If only Samuel had said, "David, it will be another twenty years before you will become king." No. Nor did Samuel prophesy, "You will be spending the next twenty years running from King Saul just to stay alive." And Samuel might have added, "Don't worry, David, this is part of your preparation." God did not lead Samuel to say anything like that.

When God commits us to service for Him, He often tells us *nothing* regarding pitfalls and disappointments along the way. We just fall into all sorts of trials and tribulations. No warning. They just come. We learn by experience. God does not lead us directly from A to Z but from A to B, B to C, etc. "One Day at a Time," as the title of a popular gospel song goes. (I am told that is the most requested song in hospitals.)

Some might ask, "Since the Spirit of the Lord came upon David in power, was he not then fit to be king?" No. His anointing needed to be refined. Success came too soon for Saul. God was going to ensure that the man after His own heart did not succeed before he was ready.

Perhaps you feel God has given you a definite anointing. You have thought that the Spirit of the Lord coming on you in power means you are "ready to go." Not necessarily. Everyone's anointing needs to be refined. Victor Hugo said, "Like the trampling of a mighty army, so is the force of an idea whose time has come." I would paraphrase that: "Like the trampling of a mighty army, so is the force of one's *anointing* whose time has come." We all tend to think we are ready merely because of a touch of God on us. The twelve disciples foolishly said to Jesus, "We are able" (Matt. 20:22, KJV). God knows the truth about us. We all need more preparation.

The evidence of David's anointing came when he killed Goliath (1 Sam. 17). It was the best thing that happened to David; it won Saul's favor. It was equally the worst thing that happened to David; it incurred Saul's wrath. But David was being prepared to be the next king. Charles Spurgeon is often quoted as saying, "If I knew I had twenty years left to live, I would spend twenty of it in preparation." If your time has not yet come, it is because you need further preparation.

In 1956 I returned to Ashland, Kentucky, from my alma mater, Trevecca Nazarene College (now Trevecca Nazarene University), with an undoubted anointing. I knew that God was going to use me one day. I knew it beyond doubt. But my father was puzzled. Why had I abandoned the theology of my old denomination if God was truly with me? I assured my father that within a year I would be totally vindicated and in a great ministry that he would be proud of. A year later I wasn't in the ministry at all. Five years later I was working as a door-to-door vacuum cleaner salesman. It wasn't until 1978—some twenty-two years later, on a train from Edinburgh, Scotland, to King's Cross station in London—that my father looked at me and said, "Son, you were right; I was wrong. I am proud of you." I'm not sure I could have coped in 1956 if I had known I would have to wait so long.

God knows our frame, always remembering we are dust (Ps. 103:14). He knows how much we can bear and therefore leads us exactly according to our need, our measure of strength, and what will be needed down the road.

I don't think David could have coped had he known in advance he would be running for his life for twenty years. One year was hard enough! But all he would go through truly was part of his preparation.

He learned a lot. He learned the meaning of *mercy* in those years. How many times did God spare David's life when a vengeful King Saul was so close to killing him? God was so merciful. This comes out in the psalms he was also writing. David could not have known that those psalms he was writing during those twenty years would be a part of the canon of Holy Scripture. He learned to be a grateful man. This too comes out in the psalms. He learned how not to grieve the Holy Spirit and that he must not try to hasten his becoming king before God's time had come. He learned also to fight and survive. He was being trained to be like a general in the military. He learned leadership and how to govern his faithful warriors. Most of all, he learned to trust God when all was utterly bleak. David was indeed a man after God's own heart.

God made sure that David would be *ready* when his time came. The day came. He turned out to be the greatest king Israel ever had. It was all worth waiting for.

Are you waiting for your time to come? God is ensuring that you do not embark on any opportunity until you are ready.

For further study: 1 Samuel 24:1–7; 26:8–11; Psalms 23; 136; Isaiah 40:31; Matthew 20:20–28

Gracious Holy Spirit, thank You for the way You refine us. Forgive me for trying to rush You. I know that time belongs to You and is in your hands. Make me patient and grateful until my time comes. In Jesus's name, amen.

_____

_____

_____

_____

_____

_____

_____

_____

_____

_____

Day 13

THE HOLY SPIRIT SPEAKS
THROUGH US

W HEN I BECAME the pastor of the Church of the Nazarene in Palmer, Tennessee, in March 1955, at the age of nineteen, I was the youngest member. There were a couple dozen children around plus a handful of slightly younger teenagers than myself. But they were not actually members. Furthermore, I had felt the divine call to preach only four months before (November 1954). My first sermon in Palmer was possibly the fifth time I ever preached at all. Feeling so inadequate and insignificant, I don't think I seriously thought that God really spoke through me in those days. Although I had nothing to do with their calling me, I honestly felt that these people in Palmer were doing me a favor by letting me be their pastor. After all, I was still a student at Trevecca Nazarene College in Nashville. It was not until a few years ago, since we moved back to Nashville, that I discovered that God had indeed used me after all. I was invited to return to Palmer and to preach there. Less than ten in the congregation had been around when I was there over fifty years before. But a lady, about sixty years of age, came up to me to say that she was actually saved as a young girl under my ministry there more than fifty years before! It was the first I knew of that.

Can you think of anything more thrilling than the thought that God actually speaks through you? After almost sixty years of ministry I never cease to be amazed that God would truly speak through me.

I think David felt that way. As he came to the end of his life, he wrote, "The Spirit of the LORD spoke through me; his word was on my tongue" (2 Sam. 23:2). He probably was referring to what he wrote rather than when he spoke, although the latter cannot be ruled out. He might also have been referring to his singing. He is referred to as "Israel's singer of songs" (v. 1) or "the sweet psalmist of Israel" (v. 1, ESV). Whatever, David became aware at the end of his life that the Holy Spirit used him by speaking, singing, or writing through him. Although David did not write Psalm 45, the opening words could surely describe him: "My tongue is the pen of a skillful writer" (v. 1).

Paul asked the Ephesians to pray for him that "words may be given" to him (Eph. 6:19; "utterance," KJV). Paul wanted that indescribable anointing whereby he did not struggle for words but that they flowed with ease and without effort. It is a marvelous phenomenon when a speaker—under the influence of the Holy Spirit—finds himself or herself uttering words that come so easily. This is the anointing. You may recall that we said the anointing is when your gift functions with ease. Therefore when one speaks and the words flow with ease, it is a wonderful moment.

There is an interesting study in the Greek language when you compare Acts 2:4 and Acts 2:14. Acts 2:4 states that the disciples spoke supernaturally in other tongues as "the Spirit enabled them," or "gave them utterance" (KJV; ESV). The Greek word is *apophthegges- thai*. It comes from *apophtheggomai*, which means to "speak out loudly and clearly." This is why everybody could hear them speaking in tongues. But all grasped what they said supernaturally in their "own native language" (v. 8). That the disciples were "enabled"— or given "utterance"—shows that their speaking in tongues flowed loudly and with ease. Now to Acts 2:14: Peter "addressed"—*apephthegzato*, from *apophtheg- gomai*—the crowd. This means he not only spoke loudly but also *with ease* with the same utterance or enablement as the disciples were given in Acts 2:4. Think about this. When Peter preached his sermon on the Day of Pentecost, he had the same help to speak in his own language that he had moments before when speaking in a different tongue. It indicates the super- natural power given to Peter that day. This word is used later when Paul said to Festus, "What I am saying [*apophtheggomai*] is true and reasonable" (Acts 26:25).

Peter said, "If anyone speaks, he should do it as one speaking the very words of God" (1 Pet. 4:11; "speaks oracles of God," ESV). So I conclude this segment where we began. When David's last words are introduced, it is written: "The oracle of David son of Jesse, the oracle of the man exalted by the Most High, the man anointed by the God of Jacob, Israel's singer of songs: The Spirit of the LORD spoke through me; his word was on my tongue" (2 Sam. 23:1–2).

What a wonderful thing to know that God can speak through us. And David wasn't perfect. This gives hope that the Holy Spirit can speak through you and me.

For further study: Psalm 45; Acts 2:1–4; Ephesians 6:10–20; 1 Peter 4:7–11

> *Glorious Holy Spirit, I want so much for You to use me, to speak through me. I know my words will not be infallible as in Holy Scripture, but use me as much as You can, knowing as You do how frail and human I am. In Jesus's name, amen.*

_____

_____

_____

_____

Day 14

THE HOLY SPIRIT DOES NOT FORSAKE US

WE HAVE SEEN that each person in the Trinity is truly and fully God. This has relevance with regard to our relationship to the Father, Son, and Holy Spirit. For example, it is written of God the Father that He "will never leave you nor forsake you" (Deut. 31:6). Jesus said before His ascension to heaven, "Surely I am with you always, to the very end of the age" (Matt. 28:20). Can we expect the same faithfulness with regard to the Holy Spirit? Yes. Jesus said of the Holy Spirit that He would be with us "forever" (John 14:16). But even if Jesus had not said that of the Holy Spirit, I would believe it is true.

We mentioned earlier that David, though a man after God's own heart and Israel's greatest king, was not perfect. His sins of adultery and murder rank at the top of the list in grievous and disgraceful sins in the Old Testament. Unlike Saul, David repented as soon as the prophet Nathan reproved him, and afterward he wrote down his prayer. It is Psalm 51. The first thing David asked for was mercy: "Have mercy on me, O God, according to your unfailing love; according to your great compassion blot out my transgressions. Wash away all my iniquity and cleanse me from me sin" (vv. 1–2). But I want to focus on these words: "Do not cast me from your presence or take your Holy Spirit from me" (v. 11). Some think this shows that the Holy Spirit leaves us when we sin because David prayed as he did—that God would not take the Holy Spirit from him. He did not pray that because the Holy Spirit leaves us when we sin; David prayed this because he *feared* this and was conscious of what he deserved. He prayed this way because the presence of God was so precious to him. To him the presence of God and the Holy Spirit came to the same thing. David was horrified at the thought he might forfeit this.

He need not have worried. "Great is your faithfulness" (Lam. 3:23). The God of the Old Testament does not leave us; Jesus the Son of God does not leave us; the Holy Spirit does not leave us. And yet the proof that the Holy Spirit had not left David is the fact that he prayed as he did. Only a person who was motivated by the Holy Spirit could pray like that! His prayer for mercy shows the Holy Spirit was with him! Praying for mercy showed his repentance. Also, pleading for mercy shows you have no bargaining power; David recognized that God could give or withhold mercy and be just either way. The entire Psalm 51 can be described with one word: repentance. That is what David was showing. The Holy Spirit was at work in him, enabling David to pray as he did. Indeed, Psalm 51 is a part of Scripture—of which the Holy Spirit is the Author! All Scripture is "God-breathed," which means inspired by the Holy Spirit (2 Tim. 3:16).

David also wrote the amazing Psalm 139. Whether he wrote this before or after his horrible sin, I don't know. In any case, David wrote: "Where can I go from your Spirit? Where can I flee from your presence? If I go up to the heavens, you are there; if I make my bed in the depths, you are there" (vv. 7–8). The King James translates the latter part of verse 8, "If I make my bed in hell." The ESV leaves the Hebrew untranslated: "If I make my bed in *Sheol*"—death, the grave. David certainly had made his bed in hell when he sinned with a high hand as he did. (*Hades* is the New Testament equivalent of *Sheol*.) If he wrote that psalm after his sin it is a testimony that God indeed had not left him.

We are all sinners. "I am a sinner—great as any, worse than many."[1] "If we claim to be without sin, we deceive ourselves and the truth is not in us. If we confess our sins, he is faithful and just and will forgive us our sins and purify us from all unrighteousness" (1 John 1:8–9). It is by the grace of God that I have not sinned as David did. I am just encouraged to know that the God of the Bible is full of mercy. Jesus said to the woman found in adultery, "Neither do I condemn you…Go now and leave your life of sin" (John 8:11). The Holy Spirit is the same; He will never leave us, but He will tell us to leave our life of sin.

For further study: 2 Samuel 12:11–14; Psalm 139; Lamentations 3:19–26; 1 John 1:7–2:2

> *O Holy Spirit, I think of the phrase, "There go I but by the grace of God." Forgive me for my sins, including my self-righteousness. Thank You for Your great mercy. In Jesus' name, amen.*

_____

_____

_____

_____

_____

_____

_____

_____

Day 15

THE HOLY SPIRIT CAN
BE PROVOKED

HAVE YOU EVER provoked the Holy Spirit? I'm afraid I have. Too often. Sometimes I feel it immediately; sometimes God waits awhile before He shows me. Whereas the Lord is "slow to anger" (Exod. 34:6), it is also true that "his wrath can flare up in a moment" (Ps. 2:12). Speaking personally, I would prefer to have the latter—when He shows His annoyance at once—to get it over with. I have also concluded that, generally speaking, the greater the sin, the longer He waits to show His anger. The Lord waited some two years before He sent Nathan the prophet to expose David's heinous sins of adultery and murder. But when Moses pleaded with the Lord not to require him to be the one to deliver the Israelites and prayed, "Please send someone else to do it," instantly the Lord's anger burned against him (Exod. 4:10–14).

The children of Israel "rebelled against the Spirit of God, and rash words came from Moses' lips" (Ps. 106:33). The ESV has a different take on his incident:

"They [the Israelites] made his spirit bitter [meaning Moses] and he spoke rashly with his lips" (although there is a footnote that it could read "they rebelled against God's Spirit"). Between these two interpretations there is to be seen both the Lord's displeasure and Moses's anger. But what Moses was feeling was righteous anger toward the children of Israel. Godly leaders sometimes carry heavy burdens and inwardly sigh with anger when their followers go astray.

The Holy Spirit never loses His temper. He mirrors joy and gladness that are always present at God's right hand (Ps. 16:11). But if we are not careful, we might unwisely show personal annoyance at the wickedness we see around us. Moses—next to Jesus—was the greatest leader of men and women in human history. But he wasn't perfect. When the Israelites gave in to folly, two things happened simultaneously: they provoked the Holy Spirit, and they made Moses angry. But because Moses was human and therefore imperfect like all of us, "he spoke rashly with his lips" (Ps. 106:33, esv). A great test of leadership is to see evil and wickedness without losing our tempers.

And yet it is difficult sometimes to tell the difference. Jesus showed righteous anger when He went into the temple and "found those who were selling oxen and sheep and pigeons, and the money-changers sitting there. And making a whip of cords, he drove them out of the temple, with the sheep and oxen.

And he poured out the coins of the money-changers and overturned their tables. And he told those who sold pigeons, 'Take these things away; do not make my Father's house a house of trade'" (John 2:14–16). Jesus had the Holy Spirit without any limit (John 3:34). He was therefore angry because the Holy Spirit was angry, and also because the Father was angry, for all Jesus ever did was carrying out the wishes of the Father (John 5:19). Whereas Jesus did not lose His temper when showing His provocation, those present may have wondered! The question is: "Can I be provoked in my spirit but not lose my temper?" Paul said, "In your anger do not sin" (Eph. 4:26).

As we will see later in this book, the Holy Spirit can be grieved. The ancient Israelites "rebelled and grieved his Holy Spirit. So he turned and became their enemy and he himself fought against them" (Isa. 63:10). James warned the early Christians, "Don't you know that friendship with the world is hatred toward God? Anyone who chooses to be a friend of the world becomes an enemy of God" (James 4:4). Martin Luther said that we must know God as an enemy before we can know Him as a friend.

God's anger toward His children is called *chastening*, or being disciplined. "The Lord disciplines those he loves" (Heb. 12:6). In any case, thankfully, His anger toward His own "lasts only a moment, but his favor lasts a lifetime; weeping may remain for a night, but rejoicing comes in the morning" (Ps. 30:5).

So have you provoked the Lord? The more serious it is, the longer He may take to show it. This is why we want to know as soon as possible if we have displeased Him. In any case, be thankful for this: if we are disciplined (and we all need it from time to time), it is because we are loved.

For further study: Numbers 20:6–13; Isaiah 63:7–10; 1 Corinthians 10:1–13; James 4:1–10

> *Blessed Holy Spirit, please show me as soon as possible when I displease You, for the last thing in the world I want is to provoke You. Thank You for countless mercies as I submit myself to You afresh today. In Jesus's name, amen.*

_____

_____

_____

_____

_____

_____

Day 16

THE HOLY SPIRIT IS OMNIPRESENT

TODAY WE TAKE a brief look at one of the attributes (characteristics) of God. The three "Big Os" are His omnipotence—that He is all-powerful; His omniscience—that He knows everything; and His omnipresence—that He is everywhere. In one of the most wonderful psalms—to which I referred earlier—David said:

> Where can I go from your Spirit? Where can I flee from your presence? If I go up to the heavens, you are there; if I make my bed in the depths, you are there. If I rise on the wings of the dawn, if I settle on the far side of the sea, even there your hand will guide me, your right hand will hold me fast.
>
> —PSALM 139:7–10

When we speak of God being omnipresent, we mean that there is nowhere God is not—in all creation, in the heavens and the earth. His glory fills the universe. "'Can anyone hide in secret places so that I cannot see him?' declares the LORD. 'Do not I fill heaven and earth?' declares the LORD" (Jer. 23:24). It is impossible to escape the presence of God. "The eyes of the LORD are everywhere, keeping watch on the wicked and the good" (Prov. 15:3). "His eyes are on the ways of men; he sees their every step. There is no dark place, no deep shadow, where evildoers can hide...He takes note of their deeds, he overthrows them in the night and they are crushed" (Job 34:21–25). Jonah foolishly thought he could "flee to Tarshish from the presence of the LORD" (Jon. 1:3, ESV). But he found that this was impossible. God was present on the ship on which he sailed. God was present in the storm that caused the panic among the sailors. And Jonah found that God was present in the belly of the fish when he persuaded the sailors to throw him into the sea, for there he prayed with all his heart, and the Lord heard him (Jon. 1:15–2:10).

There are, however, two ways by which the presence of God may be known: first, His omnipresence, which may be unconscious to us. "The heavens declare the glory of God; the skies proclaim the work of his hands...In the heavens he has pitched a tent for the sun, which is like a bridegroom coming forth from his pavilion, like a champion rejoicing to run his course. It rises at one end of the heavens and makes its circuit to the other; nothing is hidden from its heat" (Ps. 19:1, 4–6). According to Paul, the very creation speaks to all humankind to display God's glory and to expose man's hypocrisy. "What may be known about God is plain to them, because God made it plain to them. For since the creation of the world God's invisible qualities—his eternal power and divine nature—have been clearly seen, being understood from what has been made, so that men are without excuse" (Rom. 1:19–20). Preaching in Athens, Paul stated that God gives all men life and breath "so that men would seek him and perhaps reach out for him and find him, though he is not far from each one of us" (Acts 17:27).

The second way is the manifest presence of God, which may be immediately recognized. His manifest presence comes to specific people and locations by the sovereign will of God. Whereas the unconscious presence of God is not at first recognizable, His manifest presence may be seen and felt by its effect. It may result in conviction of sin (Isa. 6:5), the miraculous—sometimes called a healing presence (Luke 5:17–26), and joy (Acts 13:52). The apostle John was "in the Spirit" and saw a vision of the glorified Lord and said, "When I saw him, I fell at his feet as though dead" (Rev. 1:17). These things said, sadly there are those who might be physically present when God is showing up powerfully but be so blind and prejudiced that they miss the Holy Spirit entirely.

There are times, however, when God promises to be present, and such must be taken by faith. Jesus said, "Where two or three come together in my name, there am I with them" (Matt. 18:20). This is a word that is taken by faith. We may not *feel* His presence, but we know He is there because Jesus said so. So too when we are in a severe trial. God said, "When you pass through the waters, I will be with you" (Isa. 43:2). "For thus says the One who is high and lifted up, who inhabits eternity, whose name is Holy: 'I dwell in the high and holy place, and also with him who is of a contrite and lowly spirit, to revive the spirit of the lowly, and to revive the heart of the contrite'" (Isa. 57:15, ESV).

We should be equally thankful for both the omni-presence of the Lord and His special, manifest presence. He is everywhere whether we believe it or not. But when God's Word says He is with us, always it is a reference to the Holy Spirit—and how thankful we are for Him!

For further study: Genesis 3:8–13, ESV; Psalm 139:1–18; Luke 5:17–26; Acts 17:22–31

> *O gracious Holy Spirit, how I thank You*
> *that You are with me—even when I don't*
> *feel You present with me. Increase my*
> *discernment of Your presence lest I miss*

You when You are right before my eyes. In Jesus's name, amen.

_____

_____

_____

_____

_____

_____

_____

_____

_____

_____

Day 17

THE HOLY SPIRIT RESTS ON MESSIAH SEVEN WAYS

I WOULD LIKE TO write a book someday entitled *Verses in the Bible I Don't Understand*. There are more of these than I care for you to know! But I am going to deal with some verses now I don't fully understand. Here is one of them: "Grace and peace to you from him who is, and who was, and who is to come, and from the seven spirits before his throne" (Rev. 1:4). My dilemma is rooted specifically in the curious phrase "seven spirits of God." It is found three more times in the Book of Revelation: Revelation 3:2; 4:5; and 5:6.

I am not the only one who is perplexed with this phrase. Consider the translators, for a start. The KJV has "seven Spirits of God." The ESV has "seven spirits of God." The NIV has "seven spirits of God" with a footnote: "Or the sevenfold Spirit." Whatever does this phrase mean? One suggestion is that the seven spirits are seven angels. Angels are "ministering spirits sent to serve those who will inherit salvation" (Heb. 1:14). The problem with that view is that a Trinitarian formula is implicit in Revelation 1:4–5: "Grace and peace to you from him who is, and who was, and who is to come, and from the seven spirits before his throne, and from Jesus Christ, who is the faithful witness, the firstborn from the dead, and the ruler of the kings of the earth." In between the explicit reference to the Father and the Son is the phrase "seven spirits of God."

You will have observed that much of this devotional book is exploring various ways the Holy Spirit is active in the Old Testament. So when you come to Isaiah 11:1–3, in which you see clearly a reference to the Holy Spirit, you notice that the Spirit is linked to Messiah: "A shoot will come up from the stump of Jesse; from his roots a Branch will bear fruit" (v. 1). Jesse is the father of David. This shows that the Messiah would come from the Davidic line. There follow seven ways to which the Holy Spirit is referred: "The Spirit of the LORD will rest on him—the Spirit of wisdom and of understanding, the Spirit of counsel and of power, the Spirit of knowledge and of the fear of the Lord" (v. 2). This is the nearest I can come to understanding the four references to the seven spirits of God in the Book of Revelation.

1. *The Spirit of the Lord.* This is a reference to a general anointing upon

Jesus. He Himself quoted from Isaiah 61:1–2: "The Spirit of the Lord is on me, because he has anointed me to preach good news to the poor. He has sent me to proclaim freedom for the prisoners and recovery of sight for the blind, to release the oppressed, to proclaim the year of the Lord's favor" (Luke 4:18–19). Jesus's mission is further described in Isaiah 42:1–7.

2. *The Spirit of wisdom.* When you keep in mind that Jesus had the Holy Spirit without limit (John 3:34)—this means He had all of God there is— you can grasp why He never made an unguarded comment or put a foot wrong. He put the Pharisees to silence, so too the Sadducees (Matt. 22:34–46). Truly "one greater than Solomon" had arrived (Matt. 12:42).

3. *The Spirit of understanding.* Moses asked to know God's "ways" (Exod. 33:13). Jesus totally and perfectly understood the Father's ways. He not only understood the Father and His purpose, but Jesus also understood humankind; He knew people—how they thought and

where they were hurting. Indeed, He knew "what was in a man" (John 2:25).

4. *The Spirit of counsel.* Isaiah called Jesus "Wonderful Counselor" (Isa. 9:6). A lawyer gives advice, counsel. Jesus's counsel came without a fee and was always what people needed, whether telling Nicodemus he must be "born again" (John 3:3) or not condemning the woman found in adultery but telling her to leave her life of sin (John 8:11). Is it guidance you want? Jesus always knew the next step forward—exactly what to do now.

5. *The Spirit of power.* Jesus had power to heal every sickness and disease, to forgive sins, to cast out demons, to raise up the disabled, to stop a storm by His sheer word, to preach, and to teach. Not only that, but He actually raised Himself from the dead! "Destroy this temple, and I will raise it up in three days" (John 2:19). He guaranteed eschatological power too: as for the one who believes on the Son, "I will raise him up at the last day" (John 6:40).

6. *The Spirit of knowledge.* This knowledge of Jesus comes down essentially to one thing: He completely knew the will of the Father. This included theological, historical, cosmological, and anthropological knowledge; He was the only perfect theologian. It meant the knowledge of what to say and do—all he did and said was being directed from the Father above and was carried out perfectly (John 5:19).

7. *The Spirit of the fear of the Lord.* Jesus was not afraid of the Father; He was not afraid of anything or anybody. This refers to total obedience to the Law and the prophets. Those who truly feared the Lord honored the Law and the prophets. Jesus was the only person who kept the Law perfectly. He promised to "fulfill" the Law and the prophets (Matt. 5:17)—and did so; He could say in the end, "It is finished" (John 19:30).

For further study: 1 Kings 3:16–28; Matthew 5:17–20; 12:39–42; 2 Corinthians 5:17–21

O glorious Holy Spirit, I thank You with my whole heart that all You are was totally, completely, and perfectly resident in Jesus of Nazareth, the son of David. Grant me a greater measure of Your attributes that I might bring maximum honor to Him. In Jesus's name, amen.

_____

_____

_____

_____

_____

_____

_____

_____

_____

_____

Day 18

THE HOLY SPIRIT CANNOT BE FIGURED OUT

YOU MAY RECALL that there are basically two worldviews when it comes to faith: the secular atheist view (*seeing is believing*) and the biblical view (*believing God without the evidence*). One reason the secularist—whether he or she be a scientist, philosopher, or nurse—will not accept the God of the Bible is that they want to figure out everything. They assume if something cannot eventually be figured out, it is not worth pursuing. But I ask: Would you want a God you could actually figure out? Do you want to remove the mystery and awe that is inherent in God? Some would be quick to answer: yes. This way no God exists.

The true God cannot be fully fathomed, measured, or understood. "Who has measured the Spirit of the LORD, or what man shows him his counsel? Whom did he consult, and who made him understand? Who taught him the path of justice, and taught him knowledge, and showed him the way of understanding?"

(Isa. 40:13–14, esv). It is interesting that when this verse is quoted in the New Testament, "Spirit of the Lord" becomes "mind of the Lord." "For who has known the mind of the Lord, or who has been his counselor?" (Rom. 11:34, esv). This shows that we can figure out neither God's mind nor His Spirit. For whereas the Holy Spirit has a mind of His own, for He is a *person*, He never speaks "on his own." Like the Son, the Holy Spirit only says and does what the Father directs them to say and do (John 5:19; 16:13). There is perfect unity in the Godhead.

This is also true with the various manifestations of the Holy Spirit. The effect of His presence can result in fear, awe, praise, worship, joy, or any of the fruit or gifts of the Holy Spirit. On the Day of Pentecost the observers accused the disciples of being drunk (Acts 2:13)! And yet I know from personal firsthand observation that the Holy Spirit can still do this sort of thing. I saw a lady clearly filled with the Holy Spirit needing help to walk because of the undoubted fallout of the Holy Spirit in a service. She was laughing her head off as two people helped her into the elevator and stayed with her. This was in a hotel. There was a bar close to the auditorium where the service was being held. I have no doubt that any bystander (not in the service) would have assumed she was drunk with wine or bourbon without thinking there was anything odd about it. But if a great measure of the Holy

Spirit does that today, some Christians are shocked—if not offended! But if you were to see a DVD of the preaching of George Whitefield and the effect it sometimes had on those present—people laughing, crying, shouting, or "swooning" (the word they used then for falling down)—you could easily surmise they were drunk on alcohol.

Figure that out!

If by chance this offends you, I would gently point out that Paul said not to be drunk on wine but filled with the Spirit (Eph. 5:18), knowing as he did that the Holy Spirit may bring such joy that a bystander could think one was drunk. Does this surprise you? Wine may lead to debauchery; the Holy Spirit leads to joy and a love for the honor and glory of God. The Holy Spirit can also bring a person to the place he or she is not dominated or controlled by the opinions of people. "Fear of man will prove to be a snare" (Prov. 29:25). As we will see further below, the Holy Spirit brings freedom.

Not knowing the mind of the Lord also refers to the future. You cannot figure out in advance what He will do. When the disciples were filled with the Spirit on the Day of Pentecost, they did not know that three thousand people would be converted before the days was over, that they would shortly see miracles without Jesus being physically present, or that

Gentiles eventually would be given full membership into the church without being circumcised!

Jesus said to the Twelve, "I have much more to say to you, more than you can now bear" (John 16:12). They probably thought they were up to hearing anything Jesus could say to them, but Jesus knew better. We may *think* we want to know all that is in the future or the things God has prepared for us, but God knows best. No good thing will He withhold from those who love Him (Ps 84:11).

When Paul raised the question, "Who has known the mind of the Lord?", it was in an eschatological setting—referring partly to the future of Israel. Who knows what God is up to? And when Paul quoted the verse, "Who has been his [the Holy Spirit's] counselor?", it lets us know God doesn't need our input. Open theism (the view that God doesn't know the future and needs our advice) says that God needs counseling. Dear friend, He doesn't. He doesn't need our input, opinion, help, or aid.

I love the Holy Spirit for being exactly like He is. Don't you too?

For further study: Isaiah 55:6–11; Romans 11:25–36; 1 Corinthians 1:26–31; 1 Timothy 6:11–16

> *Omniscient Holy Spirit, I feel so small in Your presence. Forgive me for a spirit of fear, and do please open me up to letting*

*You be Yourself in my life. I humbly ask
You to take over. In Jesus's name, amen.*

_____

_____

_____

_____

_____

_____

_____

_____

_____

_____

_____

_____

_____

Day 19

THE HOLY SPIRIT GIVES DREAMS AND VISIONS

ON OCTOBER 31, 1955, while driving from Palmer to Nashville, the glory of the Lord suddenly filled the car. There was, as if literally before my eyes, Jesus at my right as I kept on driving. He was interceding to the Father for me. I never felt so loved. It was as real as the beautiful Lake Hickory I can now see as I write this book. I cannot say what was going on in the heavenlies for the next sixty miles. When I get to Heaven, I will ask for a DVD to find out. An hour later I heard Jesus say to the Father, "He wants it." The Father replied, "He can have it." The Spirit of God flooded my heart with warmth and a peace I did not know was possible for anyone to have. For some thirty seconds or so there was the face of Jesus looking at me. My theology changed before that day was over. It was the first time I had a vision.

The following month I had another vision as I was praying at my bedside in my dormitory room. It was a vision of myself preaching in a famous auditorium.

I was wearing a dark blue suit. There was a choir behind me on the platform. Each member of the choir was wearing a light gray robe. I heard no voice. There was only the vision, nothing more. But I was in awe. I got up hurriedly and went into the next room to tell this to my friend Bill. I said, "Bill, God is going to use me." He said, "I know that." But I said, "But I mean *really* use me." I was a Nazarene then. The thought of a worldwide ministry was not remotely on my radar screen. But I knew from that day that God was going to give me an international ministry one day. Over the next six to eight months I had about a dozen more visions. Some have been fulfilled, some not.

The Book of Ezekiel is full of visions. All were said to come by the Holy Spirit. "The Spirit lifted me up between earth and heaven and in visions of God he took me to Jerusalem" (Ezek. 8:3). Daniel also had visions; many of these were visions in the night, which I take to mean dreams. Joel gave a prophecy: "I will pour out my Spirit on all people. Your sons and daughters will prophesy, your old men will dream dreams, your young men will see visions" (Joel 2:28). This passage was quoted by Peter on the Day of Pentecost (Acts 2:17).

When Jesus was transfigured before Peter, James, and John on a high mountain, He called the occurrence a vision. "Tell no one the vision," He said to them (Matt. 17:9, ESV). God spoke to Ananias in a vision about the conversion of Saul of Tarsus (Acts 9:10–16). Cornelius was given a vision even before he was saved in which "he distinctly saw an angel of God" (Acts 10:3). At almost the same time Peter went into a trance, and this resulted in a vision (vv. 9–20). Paul had a vision in the night (possibly a dream) that indicated he was to preach in Macedonia (Acts 16:9–10). Paul had a similar night vision that led him to stay in Corinth another year and a half (Acts 18:9–11). Paul even refers to his own dramatic conversion as a "vision from heaven" (Acts 26:19). The Book of Revelation is the greatest vision ever.

The purpose of a vision is to show us what we need to know—often with reference to the future. Sometimes it could refer to the immediate future (Acts 10) or sometimes an event in the distant future. It may be God desiring to communicate with us intimately. Isaiah's vision showed him the glory of the Lord, his own sin, and his calling. The vision on the mountain where Jesus was transfigured demonstrated the glory of Christ and His superiority to Elijah and Moses. Peter's vision enabled him to accept Gentiles. It took something extraordinary to convince the early church that they had to overcome an extraordinary prejudice.

Paul had extraordinary "visions and revelations from the Lord" (2 Cor. 12:1). Such could breed conceit, he said, so God sent him a "thorn" in his flesh to humble him. Indeed, it was necessary because he had "surpassingly great revelations" (v. 7). These may well have included the way he learned the gospel—directly from Jesus. He wrote: "I did not receive it from any man, nor was I taught it; rather, I received it by revelation from Jesus Christ" (Gal. 1:12).

One huge caution: any vision given to you or me will not be new teaching. There will be no "new revelation." The canon of Scripture is complete; nothing will ever—ever—be added to it. Should God give a vision, it will be subsidiary to Scripture and only because you need it. By the way, I don't get visions these days. Only dreams. It must because I am old!

For further study: Daniel 10:1–9; Joel 2:28–32; Matthew 2:7–12; 2 Corinthians 12:1–10

> *Sovereign Holy Spirit, I ask for what I need*
> *for my own guidance. I thank You that I*
> *have the Bible and the Holy Spirit. I thank*
> *You for showing me all I need to know. In*
> *Jesus's name, amen.*

Day 20

THE HOLY SPIRIT MAY DO UNUSUAL THINGS

THROUGHOUT THE BIBLE are stories of the Holy Spirit doing things out of the ordinary. And He still does unusual things today.

Pastor Jack Hayford tells of flying on a plane with an Indian whom he had never met. Jack felt a sudden impulse to speak to this man in a language not his own. He felt awkward but finally obeyed the Holy Spirit. When he spoke, the Indian was astonished. Jack had spoken a word of the Lord to him in the Indian's own dialect!

I met Terry Akrill in Scotland in the summer of 2003. I had never heard of or met a man like this. He emitted an aroma of roses that came on him suddenly some five years before and never left. I could literally smell him ten feet away. Sometimes oil would flow in his hands, which augmented the aroma. He was able to convey unusual things to me by whether or not the oil came on his hands. He told me something I needed to know about Yasser Arafat in the days I was seeing the late Palestinian leader. One day he phoned with a prophetic word for our daughter, Melissa; the oil had just come on him. His prophecy was fulfilled perfectly eight years later. He is now in heaven.

I know of three cases of people rising from the dead. The people involved told me personally of these happenings. They are good, credible, and honorable men. I too know of creative miracles that took place, of very stunning prophecies that were amazingly fulfilled, and of startling exorcisms. The Holy Spirit does these things.

When Obadiah ran into Elijah unexpectedly, Obadiah was almost scared to death. This was because King Ahab had been looking high and low for Elijah for three years. Obadiah needed assurance from Elijah that he would turn himself in to Ahab, or Obadiah would be in great trouble with the king. So he asked Elijah to swear an *oath* that he would go to King Ahab because, said Obadiah, "I don't know where the Spirit of the LORD may carry you when I leave you" (1 Kings 18:12). *Carry him?* Would the Spirit of the Lord literally "carry" Elijah? Did that sort of thing happen in those days that Obadiah could reason like that? After Elijah was transported to heaven, some thought he might still be around. "Perhaps the Spirit of the LORD has picked him up and set him down on some mountain or in some valley" (2 Kings 2:16). Could this happen today?

When Arthur Blessitt preached for me at Westminster Chapel, I became enthralled with the most unusual stories he shared with me—all of them now in books he has written. Perhaps the most extraordinary was this. Arthur was on Sybuyan Island, Philippines. One day in a town called San Fernando he suddenly became extremely tired and fell into a deep sleep. While he was asleep, he was—apparently—in a town on the other side of the island called Cajidiocan, fifty miles away, giving out Jesus stickers (that said "Smile God Loves You"). Arthur had not been in Cajidiocan at all. But he did go there the next day as people begged him to return in order to pray for a dying man. He went there on a three-wheel motorcycle. When he arrived there, he was obviously recognized by the crowds. As far as the people were concerned, Arthur had been there. The chief of police even reported that a man with "long hair and a beard carrying a cross" was in Cajidiocan, when in fact Arthur was asleep in San Fernando fifty miles away. Arthur knew he had not been in Cajidiocan at all. He couldn't have been there. First, he was asleep in San Fernando fifty miles away from there. Second, it was a three-day walk carrying the cross to get there. But when he arrived in Cajidiocan the next day on the three-wheel motorcycle, the streets were lined with people waiting to see him. Children wearing Jesus stickers came up to him, which "shows" Arthur had been in Cajidiocan the day before! Arthur now knew these reports must be true and that it wasn't a dream or vision. The day before he had been somehow...there. "I don't know how to explain how or why this happened," he said to me on the phone as I was writing this chapter. In all of his experiences of carrying the cross all over the world, this account was unique. "It only happened once"— on a remote island where people on the whole did not read or write. He has walked the equivalent of one and a half times around the world (he holds the Guinness Book of Records for the longest walk).

But there is more. You will recall that Arthur was being taken on a three-wheel motorcycle from San Fernando to Cajidiocan to pray for a dying man. The man had been given the last rites by the local priest. When Arthur arrived, he saw a man in an upstairs window looking down at him. The man ran down the stairs to see who he thought was Jesus! The man thought he had died and was in heaven seeing Jesus. It was the dying man Arthur came to pray for, healed before Arthur got to him. The man spoke English. He even translated for Arthur as he preached the gospel to these people. Arthur told me, "Everyone I prayed for was healed"—on a remote island in the Philippines. Why doesn't God do that in America or Britain? You can read more details on Arthur's website.

I have more stories—not about Arthur but equally

unusual—I could relate. But I fear you wouldn't believe them! Nor do I have permission to tell them.

For further study: 1 Kings 17:7–24; 2 Kings 7:1–20; Acts 9:32–43; 1 Corinthians 2:8–9

> *Omnipotent Holy Spirit, how I thank You that Jesus Christ is the same yesterday, today, and forever. I am so glad You can do extraordinary things today just as You did in the past. Please come down again in our day that the world may see how real You are. In Jesus's name, amen.*

Day 21

THE HOLY SPIRIT WORKS SUPERNATURALLY

ONE OF THE best descriptions of the Holy Spirit in the Old Testament is found in these words: "'Not by might nor by power, but by my Spirit,' says the LORD Almighty" (Zech. 4:6). These words were addressed to Zerubbabel the governor of Judah. He was told how the rebuilding of the temple would be accomplished. "Might" probably refers to collective strength; "power" means an individual's strength. In other words, the rebuilding of the temple would be carried out *supernaturally*—not something that can be explained at the natural level. The rebuilding of the temple would be a supernatural enterprise. For once the Holy Spirit is brought in, it means that one has crossed over from the natural to the supernatural.

This does not mean that we do not get involved. We do. But all we have to do is to obey the Lord. Then the Holy Spirit moves in and does the rest. For example, God waited for Moses to lift up his staff when the children of Israel came upon the Red Sea with Pharaoh's army chasing them. That's all he had to do. God promised him: "The Lord will fight for you; you need only to be still...Raise your staff and stretch out your hand over the sea to divide the water so that the Israelites can go through the sea on dry ground" (Exod. 14:14–16). Then Moses stretched out his hand over the sea, and all that night the Lord drove the sea back with a strong east wind and turned it into dry land. The Israelites went through the sea on dry land, with a wall of water on their right and on their left. All Moses did was to raise his staff and hand. That was the natural side. The Holy Spirit did the supernatural part.

In a battle between Israel and the Amalekites, strange as this may seem, "as long as Moses held up his hands, the Israelites were winning, but whenever he lowered his hands, the Amalekites were winning." When Moses grew tired, Aaron and Hur held his hands up, "one on one side, one on the other— so that his hands remained steady till sunset," and the Amalekites were defeated (Exod. 17:11–13). God intervened supernaturally. But it was connected to Moses's hands being lifted.

This pattern continued after Israel entered the land of Canaan. Sometimes God asks us to do strange things that make no sense to us. God told Joshua to have the children of Israel march around the city of

Jericho every day for six days. Then on the seventh day they were to march around the city seven times, with the priests blowing trumpets. Then the people were to give a loud shout, which resulted in the walls of Jericho collapsing. They did this as they were commanded. They may have felt stupid. Walking around the city. Quietly. With no weapons. But on the seventh day after circling the city seven times, *the people gave a loud shout*, and the walls collapsed (Josh. 6:1–20). They did the easy part; God did the rest.

God later told Joshua, "Hold out toward Ai the javelin that is in your hand, for into your hand I will deliver the city" (Josh. 8:18). The result was a total victory for Israel. The Holy Spirit did it. But Joshua had to hold the javelin and point it toward the place of battle. Centuries later King Jehoshaphat was challenged by the Ammonites. The Spirit of the Lord came upon Jahaziel, who said, "The battle is not yours, but God's" (2 Chron. 20:15). The Israelites did nothing but sing to the Lord. "As they began to sing and praise, the LORD set ambushes against the men of Ammon and Moab and Mount Seir who were invading Judah, and they were defeated" (v. 22). The victory was wholly supernatural but was nonetheless inseparably connected to their singing to the Lord.

This is exactly what was meant by the prophet's word to Zerubbabel. The people still had to get the materials for the temple. They had to rebuild the foundation. They had to lay the stones. But it all *happened with ease.* This is the essence of the anointing of the Holy Spirit; it enables one's gift to function with ease.

John Wesley said that God does nothing but in answer to prayer. I'm not sure I believe this entirely, but the Lord did say, "In all your ways acknowledge him, and he will make your paths straight" (Prov. 3:6). This verse is preceded by a crucial truth that we should remember every single day of our lives: "Trust in the LORD with all your heart and lean not on your own understanding" (v. 5). Our understanding may suggest that God's ways don't make sense. He replies, "My thoughts are not your thoughts, neither are your ways my ways…As the heavens are higher than the earth, so are my ways higher than your ways and my thoughts than your thoughts" (Isa. 55:8–9).

We do our part—might and power, operating at the natural level. God does His part—by the Holy Spirit, doing the supernatural. How foolish we are to argue with His ways.

For further study: Exodus 14:13–31; 2 Chronicles 20:5–23; John 6:63; 2 Corinthians 9:6–11

> *Gracious Holy Spirit, thank You for being just as You are. Please forgive me for doubting Your Holy Word and Your infinite power. In Your mercy grant me grace*

to help by not leaning on my own under-standing but to trust You entirely. In Jesus's name, amen.

_____

_____

_____

_____

_____

_____

_____

_____

_____

_____

_____

_____

_____

Day 22

THE HOLY SPIRIT IS THE
SPIRIT OF TRUTH

D O YOU EVER wonder if integrity as a virtue is perishing from the earth? Whatever happened to sheer honesty? Just being truthful—publicly, privately. Saying what you mean and meaning what you say. Keeping your word.

The God of the Bible is a God of integrity. It is impossible for God to lie (Heb. 6:18). Our Lord Jesus Christ has transparent integrity. The Holy Spirit is totally, thoroughly, and completely honest. Jesus called Him the Spirit of truth (John 14:17).

As for Jesus, He said of Himself that He is "the way and the *truth* and the life" (v. 6, emphasis added), and so equally the Holy Spirit is truth. As it is impossible for God to lie, never forget that the Holy Spirit is *incapable* of lying to you. He will never deceive you.

Jesus Himself was full of grace and "truth" (John 1:14). Truth means fact. It means what is reliable. What Jesus does and says can be proved, and He will not let you be ashamed. When a miracle was performed, the enemy of truth was forced to say, "We cannot deny it" (Acts 4:16). Jesus is transparent integrity. Today we sometimes use the expression "the real deal." It is what people want to see in leaders, what people long for in relationships—no deceit, no infidelity, but honesty and trustworthiness. That is what we want in a friend—pure gold, the real thing.

Jesus is that. The God of the Bible is that—His words are "trustworthy" (2 Sam. 7:28), "true, and righteous altogether" (Ps. 19:9, ESV). And so virtually the first thing Jesus said about the Holy Spirit was that He is "the Spirit of truth." This means genuineness, trustworthiness, faithfulness, and integrity. It also means theological truth. The Holy Spirit will never lead you to error. What He reveals you can believe and stake your life on.

To put it another way, the Holy Spirit is the opposite of the devil. Jesus said of Satan: "There is no truth in him...for he is a liar and the father of lies (John 8:44, ESV). He is incapable of integrity and honesty. He exists to deceive. Do you know the feeling of being deceived? To know what it is to embrace a person, recommend them, put your reputation on the line for them—then find out you were deceived? It can be very painful.

Jesus said to Pilate, "Everyone on the side of truth listens to me" (John 18:37). Pilate responded by asking, "What is truth?" (v. 38). Did Pilate ask that question because he wanted an answer? Was he being cynical? Was he suggesting that he didn't know what truth is and doubted whether anybody knows the truth? Jesus meant that there is truth that is objectively true—that is, factual.

Dr. Francis Schaeffer used a phrase: "true truth." He believed Scripture is *true truth,* that it is trustworthy and faithful. Jesus believed in what can be called propositional revelation—that there is a body of truth that does not change. So when Jesus said that everyone who is on the side of truth listens to Him, it is because all who want what is *really* true and *objectively* true will embrace Jesus Himself and His words. John said, "Whoever knows God listens to us; but whoever is not from God does not listen to us. This is how we recognize the Spirit of truth and the spirit of falsehood" (1 John 4:6). Those, then, who have the Holy Spirit in them will be drawn to truth wherever it is and will be willing to test their findings and opinion by Scripture.

In a word: if you have the Holy Spirit, you will believe that Jesus Christ the Son of God is the true God and that the Bible is infallibly true.

A good question to put to yourself is this: What would you go to the stake for? What would you die for? In my old age I have concluded that the only thing I will preach is what I would die for. If it isn't worth dying for, it isn't worth preaching—or believing.

Granted, there are gray areas where we might have to give an opinion on—e.g., eschatology (doctrine of last things) or ecclesiology (your view of the church or sacraments). I wouldn't die for these. But I would go to the stake for what I believe about the person of Jesus Christ, salvation, the Bible, and the Holy Spirit. I would go to the stake for what I am writing in this book.

"You have an anointing from the Holy One…and all of you know the truth" (1 John 2:20). The Holy Spirit is the Spirit of *truth*, and that means we will be kept from error as long as we have a determination to do the will of God. For over fifty years I have kept John 7:17 in mind: "If anyone chooses to do God's will, he will find out whether my teaching comes from God." This also shows that your personal relationship with God—whether you want to do His will or not—will determine what you believe.

The Holy Spirit will never mislead you. You don't need to be afraid of Him. He may not be "safe," but He is "good."

For further study: Malachi 2:5–8; John 14:6–17; 17:17–19; Philippians 4:6–8

> *Precious Holy Spirit, I am so thankful that You are the Spirit of truth. This way I know that You will never lead me in the wrong direction, that I can follow You and know I am not being deceived. Thank You*

*for being just like You are. In Jesus's name,
amen.*

_____

_____

_____

_____

_____

_____

_____

_____

_____

_____

_____

Day 23

THE HOLY SPIRIT, USING PEOPLE, WROTE THE BIBLE

ALL SCRIPTURE IS God-breathed and is useful for teaching, rebuking, correcting and training in righteousness" (2 Tim. 3:16). "For prophecy never had its origin in the will of man, but men spoke from God as they were carried along by the Holy Spirit" (2 Pet. 1:21).

What you believe about the Bible is absolutely crucial to your spiritual life. As long as you believe that Holy Scripture *is* the word of God, you can be protected from heresy (theological error). *Heresy* is a word we don't hear much about these days. Some think theological exactness is less and less important. Wrong. It has never been more important in the history of the Christian church than it is today. Back in the 1950s there emerged a point of view in seminaries and universities called neoorthodoxy, "new" orthodoxy. The champions of this were men like Karl Barth, Emil Brunner, Paul Tillich, and Rudolf Bultmann. They sounded good—at first. Many young students became enamored with them. I myself flirted with this for a while. I was taught by professors who embraced neoorthodoxy. God in His mercy kept me from succumbing. One of my professors lived in Brunner's home (who lived in Zurich, Switzerland) and carried notes daily from Brunner to Barth (who lived in Basel). One premise of neoorthodoxy is that the Bible "contains" the Word of God rather than that the Bible *is* the Word of God.

I have watched the pattern of those who imbibed this teaching. A typical scenario was this: they first were attracted to Barth or Brunner. They went from Barth to Tillich—the existentialist who called faith "ultimate concern." He said you could be an atheist and still have faith because God was the "ground of all being." They then moved from Tillich to Bultmann, who said the miracles reported in the Bible are "myths." They then ended up in "process theology," the notion that truth is not an unchangeable body of propositions but always changing. God does not even know the future but is "enriched" by creation and waits for our input in order to know what to do next. Yes, I watched students come to seminary who had always assumed the Bible is true but ended up disillusioned with a "faulty document." They either became hopeless theological liberals or abandoned the ministry entirely. It makes one weep. When you hear of people embracing open theism (process theology in evangelical dress) and universalism (everybody will be saved and none go to hell), it shows how widespread this has become. It goes back to your view of Holy Scripture.

John Calvin gave to the church the teaching of the "internal testimony of the Holy Spirit," namely, how you know the Bible is the Word of God. It is the Holy Spirit who witnesses in your heart that the Bible is absolutely true. With this was the very important teaching of the "analogy of faith," based upon Romans 12:6 (*analogia*, usually translated "proportion"). We must prophesy or teach according to the "proportion" of our faith. This meant comparing Scripture with Scripture and staying in Scripture. This way one discovers how amazing and consistent the Bible is.

When I was ordained to the ministry, Dr. N. B. Magruder asked me, "Which is more important—the external or internal witness—when it comes to knowing the Bible is true?" Answer: internal witness. External witness refers to what *people* say about the Bible; for example, archeologists or New Testament critics. The only safe route is *the way of the Holy Spirit*; His own witness enables you to know you are never going to be deceived when you are convinced in your heart the Bible is true and trustworthy. I can tell you, I would never have made it as an expositor of Scripture over the last sixty years of preaching were I not totally convinced that every word of Scripture is true and must be taken with the gravest seriousness. It is what has saved me from becoming a liberal.

Jesus had the same view of Scripture that Paul and Peter held to, namely, that the Holy Spirit wrote the Old Testament. Jesus asked the Pharisees (a question they could not answer), "How is it then that David, *speaking by the Spirit*, calls him [Christ] 'Lord'? For he says, 'The Lord said to my Lord: "Sit at my right hand until I put your enemies under your feet." If then David calls him "Lord," how can he be his son?'"(Matt. 22:43–45, emphasis added). My point is, Jesus said that David was able to write as he did because the *Holy Spirit*—in 1000 BC—enabled him to do so. And, as we also saw earlier, it was the testimony of the early church. When being persecuted, they prayed to the Lord and said, "You *spoke by the Holy Spirit* through the mouth of your servant David: 'Why do the nations rage and the peoples plot in vain?'" (Acts 4:25, emphasis added).

One more thing in this connection: The canon of Holy Scripture is closed. It is final. Absolute. Incontrovertible. It is God's complete and final revelation. No word that will come in the future will be equal to the Bible in level of inspiration. This means that any *"leading," prophetic word, word of knowledge,* or *vision* one may have today *must cohere with Holy Scripture.* If it doesn't, it must be rejected. The main reason that King Saul became yesterday's man and was rejected by God was because he thought he was above the Word of God. When he offered the burnt offerings, he knew he was going against Moses's mandate that only the priest called of God could offer burnt offerings. And yet he claimed to have been "compelled" to do it (1 Sam. 13:12). Whenever a person claims to speak for God, claiming "The Lord told me"—and it goes against Scripture, you may safely, comfortably, and most assuredly reject that person's word, no matter how credible that person may seem!

The Holy Spirit takes responsibility for the authorship of the Bible. He used people of course. But the *buck* stops with the Holy Spirit. The same Holy Spirit may speak today at various levels. But no level of inspiration will equal the inspiration of the Bible—ever.

For further study: John 5:39–47; Acts 4:24–31; 2 Timothy 3:15–16; 2 Peter 1:21

> *Blessed Holy Spirit, I thank You for the Bible—the infallible Word of God. I thank You that You wrote it—using people. Please dwell in me in ever-increasing measure in order that Your Word will be more and more real to me. In Jesus's name, amen.*

Day 24

THE HOLY SPIRIT IS
OUR TEACHER

I HAVE HAD SEVERAL mentors, probably about ten. I have often wished I could write a book about them. The problem is, they are not well known, and writing such a book would mean more to me than the reader. But the notable exception is Dr. Martyn Lloyd-Jones. He taught me through his books for years and then spoon-fed me week after week during my first four years at Westminster Chapel. He was my chief mentor. He taught me the difference between the direct and indirect witness of the Spirit. More than anyone else, he taught me how to think. That said, anyone's greatest teacher is the Holy Spirit.

"He will teach you all things," said Jesus (John 14:26, ESV). "You do not need anyone to teach you. But as his anointing teaches you about all things and as that anointing is real, not counterfeit…remain in him" (1 John 2:27).

The Holy Spirit is our teacher in basically two ways: directly and indirectly—a most important concept.

If He teaches us directly, then, "you do not need anyone to teach you." The Holy Spirit is very capable of teaching us in that fashion, and it is a wonderful thing to have happen. This is what happened to me when driving in my car on October 31, 1955 (as I discussed in Day 19). The things I was taught directly had previously been alien to me—for example, that I was eternally saved and chosen from the foundation of the world. I could not have thought that up in my own mind. I was taught the opposite—that such teaching was actually "born in hell" (I am not joking). So how did I come to it? By the direct teaching of the Holy Spirit.

Whether it be the indirect or direct teaching, the Holy Spirit only teaches us what we are able to take in. Jesus had much more He could teach the Twelve but knew they were not able to absorb any more (John 16:12). Not only that, but also Holy Spirit never makes us feel guilty when we are slow to grasp things. My first-grade teacher (when I was six years old) would stand behind me and shake my shoulders suddenly in front of the rest of the class when I read a word or sentence improperly. I have had serious trouble reading and concentrating when I read ever since. I was sick at home and unable to attend school the early days of my first algebra class. The teacher never offered to help me catch up, and the result was that I never—ever—got it right when it came to algebra.

My basketball coach once threw a basketball at me that hit me hard in the pit of my stomach and left me breathless for a while. I was expecting a gentle toss from him. I was afraid to let him teach me after that. But Jesus never makes mistakes like that.

The indirect teaching refers to the way the Holy Spirit *applies* what we read or hear. It is when the Spirit applies the Word of God as we read it. It is when the Spirit applies preaching, teaching, a blog, a poem, a loving word of encouragement from a friend, what we read in a book, or when we sing a hymn or chorus. As it happens, this very morning in my quiet time I sang the hymn "Be Still, My Soul" to the tune "Finlandia." Only God (and Louise, who was with me) knew what those words meant to me on this particular day. It was as though they were penned for me! The Holy Spirit was at work applying this great hymn.

Chastening, or disciplining, is the Holy Spirit's indirect teaching. The word *chastening* comes from a word that means enforced learning—whatever it takes to get our attention. It is God's Plan B in dealing with us. Plan A is that we should listen to God through His Word. That is the best way of having our spiritual problem solved! Plan B is when He resorts to measures more painful than having to obey His Word—as when we are required to go outside our comfort zone. The Holy Spirit may use sickness, financial reverse, the withholding of vindication, or losing a friend. Or even being swallowed up by a great fish, as Jonah learned. Whom the Lord loves He disciplines (Heb. 12:6). But He knows how much we can bear.

The Holy Spirit is our best and only reliable teacher. In fact, He is the only teacher who ultimately matters. Whatever teaching you hear or read (including this book), whoever the preacher or teacher, if the Spirit does not apply it and witness it to your heart (which He is most capable of doing), you should learn to hold that teaching in abeyance—if not dismiss it.

Caution: whether you are learning from Him directly or indirectly, the Holy Spirit only witnesses to and leads to the *truth*. We have seen that the best of human teachers make mistakes. Our best mentors are not infallible. We must all be like the people of Berea who "examined the Scriptures [the Old Testament, in this case] every day to see if what Paul said was true" (Acts 17:11). In those days, Paul was a *nobody*; he did not have the stature then that he has today. Anyone who says to you, "Believe it because I say it," is doing you no favor and is probably insecure in himself.

The Holy Spirit is not insecure. He has nothing to prove. He is only looking out for you.

For further study: Exodus 33:7–23; Psalm 119:65–72; 2 Timothy 4:1–5; Hebrews 5:11–6:2

*O Holy Spirit, my greatest teacher, thank
You for Your patience with me. I feel I have
so much to learn. Thank You for Your
patience. Don't give up on me. Teach me
all I can know that will bring great honor
and glory to the most high and all wise
God. In Jesus's name, amen.*

_____

_____

_____

_____

_____

_____

_____

_____

_____

Day 25

THE HOLY SPIRIT CAN BE GRIEVED

ONE OF THE most neglected teachings nowadays is the Christian's inheritance. Every believer is called to come into his or her inheritance. Some do; some don't (sadly). The word *inheritance* may be used interchangeably with "reward" (1 Cor. 3:14), "prize" (1 Cor. 9:27), or "crown" (2 Tim. 4:8). Those who come into their inheritance here below will receive a reward at the judgment seat of Christ (2 Cor. 5:10). Those who blow away their inheritance will be saved, but by fire with no reward (1 Cor. 3:15). A reward was of great importance to Paul. He said he kept his body under control lest having to preach to others he himself be rejected for the prize (1 Cor. 9:27).

You come into your inheritance by careful obedience to the word of God—walking in the light, resisting temptation, forgiving your enemies, and honoring God in thought, word, and deed. It can be summed up this way: find out what *grieves* the Holy Spirit and *don't do that*. The most important teaching

I discovered in my twenty-five years at Westminster Chapel was the importance of not grieving the Holy Spirit. Your inheritance below—seeing God's will fulfilled in your life and finishing well—is assured to the degree the Holy Spirit is *ungrieved*.

"Do not grieve the Holy Spirit of God, with whom you were sealed for the day of redemption" (Eph. 4:30). You will recall from an early segment in this book that the Holy Spirit is a person. He can be *grieved*. The Greek word *lupeo* can mean, "get your feelings hurt." What hurts the Holy Spirit's feelings? Chiefly, bitterness. The next thing Paul says is, "Get rid of all bitterness, rage and anger, brawling and slander, along with every form of malice. Be kind and compassionate to one another, forgiving each other, just as in Christ God forgave you" (Eph. 4:31–32).

I have written an entire book on this subject, called *The Sensitivity of the Spirit*. Not sensitivity *to* the Spirit, important though that is; this book deals with how sensitive the *person* of the Holy Spirit Himself is. I wanted to call my book *The Hyper-Sensitivity of the Spirit*, but my publisher talked me out of it, knowing people would have no idea what this meant. When we refer to a person who is overly sensitive, it is not a compliment. But like it or not, that is the way the way the Holy Spirit is! It is important that you grasp this—how easy it is to grieve Him, to hurt His feelings. You might say, "He shouldn't be like that." All

I know is, this is the way He is, and He is the only Holy Spirit we have! When you think about this— that anger, losing your temper, shouting when you get frustrated, speaking impatiently to or unkindly of a person, holding a grudge, or pointing the finger— these things grieve the Holy Spirit!

The problem is, with so many people these things don't seem to bother them! They should. If we are conscious of the sensitivity *of* the Holy Spirit, we will develop an acute sensitivity *to* Him—and be able (in ever-increasing measure) to hear His voice. Before he became king, David needed to learn about this. When he had a chance to get vengeance upon King Saul, who wanted to kill him, David wisely turned down the opportunity. But he did one thing he thought was harmless; namely, he cut off a piece of the king's robe. Afterward he was "conscience-stricken" for doing this (1 Sam. 24:5). He never repeated that sin again. That is what I mean by my earlier comment about finding out what grieves the Holy Spirit and *don't do that*. In any case, we must learn to narrow the time gap between sin and repentance. If we develop an acute sensitivity to the Holy Spirit's ways, we will be able to *feel* it when we grieve Him. When I sense what exactly grieves the Spirit, I am able not to repeat this. As I said earlier, the chief way to grieve Him is by bitterness and unforgiveness. Avoiding bitterness, holding a grudge, and losing one's temper come by living in love—keeping no record of wrongs (1 Cor. 13:5).

In 1974 my family and I visited Corrie ten Boom (1892–1983) in Holland. I asked her, "Is it true that you are a charismatic?" Without saying yes or no, she bluntly replied: "First Corinthians 12 and 1 Corinthians 14. But don't forget 1 Corinthians 13." It was a shrewd way of saying we need both the gifts and the fruit of the Holy Spirit.

When it comes to grieving the Holy Spirit, I'm sorry, but He will not bend the rules for any of us. It does not matter how high your profile is, how educated you are, how much you pray and read your Bible, or how long you have been a Christian. If you or I hold a grudge, snap back at our spouse, point the finger, or speak evil of some person (even if it is true), the Dove—the Holy Spirit—will be grieved. The good news is that we do not forfeit our salvation when we grieve the Spirit. Why? Because we are sealed for the day of redemption (Eph. 4:30). The bad news is that our anointing diminishes—that is, the sense of His presence. We cannot think as clearly, Bible reading becomes boring, insights into Scripture are withheld, and we become irritable. Grieving the Holy Spirit isn't worth it!

Is there anybody you have not forgiven? Are you holding a grudge toward a person who has hurt you, lied about you, or who has been unjust? Forgive them!

Do it now. You may ask, "How may I know I have totally forgiven them?" First, don't tell anyone what they did to you. Second, don't let them feel afraid of you. Third, help them to forgive themselves. Fourth, let them save face (instead of rubbing their noses in it). Fifth, don't reveal their most embarrassing secret. Sixth, do it now, again tomorrow, and ten years from now. Total forgiveness is a life commitment. Finally, pray for them, sincerely asking God to bless them.

Do these things, and the *ungrieved* Holy Spirit will descend upon you and give you peace, joy, and clear thinking. Best of all, you will come into your inheritance.

For further study: Genesis 45:1–8; 1 Samuel 24:1–7; Ephesians 4:29–5:5; 1 Peter 2:21–25

> *Precious Holy Spirit, I am so sorry that I have grieved You. I ask for Your forgiveness. And I now ask You to bless that person who has hurt me. Thank You for this word from You, and thank You for convicting me of my sin. In Jesus's name, amen.*

_____

_____

_____

_____

Day 26

THE HOLY SPIRIT CAN
BE QUENCHED

THE HOLY SPIRIT is depicted in the New Testament in at least five ways—the dove, fire, oil, wind, and water. Water cleanses. It is said that our bodies are washed "with pure water" (Heb. 10:22). The dove relates to the sensitivity of the Holy Spirit. The dove is a shy, sensitive bird. When the dove came down on Jesus and *remained* (John 1:32–33), it showed that Jesus never grieved the Spirit, as I show in *The Sensitivity of the Spirit*. As for oil, this is something one has to make preparation for. Moreover, the wise virgins took oil in their vessels; the foolish did not (Matt. 25:3–4). As for the wind depicting the Spirit, wind cannot be controlled; it is out of our hands. When the wind chooses to blow, nothing will stop it. In any case, there are at least three references to wind in the New Testament: (1) on the Day of Pentecost (Acts 2:2); (2) Jesus's words to Nicodemus, "The wind blows wherever it pleases" (John 3:8); and (3) to the inspiration of the Holy Scriptures (2 Tim. 3:16).

Quenching the Spirit refers to fire—fire that is already burning. You cannot quench fire by pouring water on what isn't there. Therefore quenching the Spirit implies that the Spirit is at work, but that one can quench Him; that is, put out the fire. That said, I think it is possible to quench the Spirit before He has had opportunity to work, perhaps like pouring water on wood before it can burn, as I will show below.

There is only one explicit reference to quenching the Spirit in the New Testament: "Do not quench the Spirit" (1 Thess. 5:19, ESV). "Don't put out the Holy Spirit's fire" (NIRV). What is the difference between grieving the Spirit and quenching the Spirit? They almost certainly overlap. But if there is a difference, it is probably this: we grieve the Spirit mostly by our relationships with one another—like judging and unforgiveness; we quench the Spirit mainly when we are prejudiced against the way the Spirit may be manifesting Himself or by not respecting His presence. It is often fear that lies behind quenching the Holy Spirit. But it could also be smugness. It is largely Christians who quench the Holy Spirit; after all, the words "do not quench the Spirit" are addressed to Christians. But you don't need to be saved to quench the Spirit.

All the examples that follow had in common that they quenched the Spirit. First, the Gnostics. They were never converted and were a great threat to the

Christian faith. They did not believe that Jesus Christ had come in the flesh (1 John 2:19–22). They came into the church through the back door and ruthlessly quenched the Spirit by infiltrating the fellowship (Jude 4). They were "blemishes at your love feasts, eating with you without the slightest qualms" (Jude 12).

Another enemy of the church were the Judaizers. These were Jews who made professions of faith but insisted that all Gentiles be circumcised. They hated Paul and all he stood for. They not only quenched the Spirit but almost ruined the Galatians. Anybody who superimposes the Mosaic Law on believers seriously risks quenching the Holy Spirit. The Galatians, though they were clearly converted, were in a terrible bondage. This is why Paul was adamant: "It is for freedom that Christ has set us free. Stand firm, then, and do not let yourselves be burdened again by a yoke of slavery" (Gal. 5:1). For "where the Spirit of the Lord is, there is freedom" (2 Cor. 3:17).

It was definitely true Christians who quenched the Holy Spirit in the church of Corinth. They met in homes to celebrate the Lord's Supper. But certain middle-class Christians took over. They did not bother to wait for the poorer members who had to work late and therefore arrived after the Lord's Supper was over (1 Cor. 11:21). God judged these middle-class Christians with weakness, illness, and death (v. 30). Ananias and Sapphira quenched the Spirit, which resulted in their deaths, when they lied in the presence of God (Acts 5:1–11).

In my book *Holy Fire* I talk about a false teaching called "cessationism"—a manufactured theory that claims that the miraculous "ceased" some two thousand years ago by God's own decree. These people maintain that the Holy Spirit does not, will not, or cannot manifest today through the gifts of the Spirit. Therefore when individuals adhere to cessationism, the Holy Spirit is virtually quenched before He is given an opportunity to show His power; it is like pouring water on wood that cannot burn.

Don't be threatened by the Holy Spirit. Some would say that the Holy Spirit is a "gentleman." But I'm not sure I always agree with that! Whereas I am sure you don't need to be threatened by Him, He still may not be as *nice* as some might hope. Dr. Lloyd-Jones said often that the problem with the ministry today is that it has "too many nice men" in it. The Holy Spirit may require something of you that was not on your radar screen. Back in 1982 I made the decision to give up my aspiration of being a great theologian and instead be willing to take to the streets, give out tracts—not that I am suggesting they are mutually exclusive! I began to talk to complete strangers and passers-by about the Lord. It was so embarrassing! But I never looked back.

So I do not say God will not require something of

you that leads you out of your comfort zone. You may indeed have to leave your comfort zone. But I can promise this: follow the Holy Spirit by being totally open to Him; you will be forever thankful. In any case, please do not quench the Holy Spirit—or pour water on wood so that the fire cannot burn.

For further study: Acts 8:18–24; 1 Corinthians 11:17–21, 27–32; Galatians 3:1–5; Jude 4–13

> *O Holy Spirit, please overrule in my life that I will never quench the fire that You have caused to burn. Let me never pour water on wood You may want to ignite. I pray on bended knee that You will come unquenched into my heart and stay there without any hindrance from me. In Jesus's name, amen.*

_____

_____

_____

_____

_____

Day 27

THE HOLY SPIRIT
CONVICTS OF SIN

H E WILL CONVICT the world concerning sin and righteousness and judgment" (John 16:8, ESV). Only the Holy Spirit can make us see our sin, show us the need for righteousness, and the urgency of the gospel—that there is judgment. A person cannot feel convicted of these things on his or her own. It takes the Spirit to shake us rigid.

This is true before and after our conversion. We cannot see our sin or the seriousness of unbelief before our conversion—we are all so self-righteous. It requires the Holy Spirit to make us see the painful truth—that we have grieved Him by self-righteousness and unbelief and are going to have to give an account of our lives at the judgment seat of Christ. Even after conversion we must beware of self-righteousness. This is why John said, writing to Christians, "If we claim to be without sin, we deceive ourselves and the truth is not in us" (1 John 1:8). It is also why it is good to pray the Lord's Prayer daily—recalling the petition,

"Forgive us our sins, for we also forgive everyone who sins against us" (Luke 11:4).

The Spirit shows us our sin but also leads us to see the need for righteousness—of which there are two sorts:

1. Righteousness imputed to us when we believe the gospel—called saving faith

2. Righteousness imparted to us when we "continue to live in him" (Col. 2:6)— called persistent faith

Righteousness is connected to Jesus's ascension ("I am going to the Father, where you can see me no longer," John 16:10) partly because the preaching of the gospel did not begin until Jesus died, rose from the grave, and ascended to the Father's right hand.

But what is the "judgment" of which the Spirit promises to convict us? Two things. First, it is a reminder of the wrath of God. After Paul said that he was "unashamed of the gospel" (Rom. 1:16), he gave the real reason people need to be saved: "The wrath of God is being revealed from heaven against all ungodliness and wickedness of men" (Rom. 1:18). The issue is this: Why be a Christian? Some say, "You will be so much better off." "You will be a happier person." "You can enjoy prosperity." "It will help your marriage." And on and on come the various suggestions. But the *real* reason a person should be a Christian is owing to the wrath of God. The earliest message of the New Testament was from John the Baptist, warning us to "flee from the coming wrath" (Matt. 3:7).

Second, it is a reference to the Final Day—when the Judge of all the earth shall do right. (See Genesis 18:25.) Satan is the cause of all the evil and injustice in this world. The death of Jesus took Satan by surprise (1 Cor. 2:8) and not only spelled his downfall but also forecast the day of his judgment. Death was defeated by Jesus's death (Heb. 2:14), which is why Jesus said, "The prince of this world now stands condemned" (John 16:11). People often ask, "Is there no justice in this world?" Answer: Sometimes there is, but don't count on it. "Life's not fair," said John F. Kennedy. But one day God will openly bring about Satan's demise. God will explain the reason for evil and suffering. Everything will be put under Jesus's feet. Satan himself will be "thrown into the lake of burning sulfur" (Rev. 20:10). The Holy Spirit convicts of this truth, testifying that Satan stands condemned but also that judgment is coming.

For this reason, we "all" must stand before the judgment seat of Christ and give an account of the things done in the body, whether good or bad (2 Cor. 5:10). The Holy Spirit therefore convicts of the final judgment. The affect this should have on us is godly fear. As soon as Paul mentioned standing before the judgment, he mentioned the "fear" of the Lord ("knowing therefore the terror of the Lord," 2 Cor. 5:11, KJV). The reference to judgment also points to the neglected teaching of eternal punishment. When Paul witnessed before Felix, he spoke of "judgment to come." Felix was afraid. He trembled (Acts 24:25, KJV). In times of great revival there is often a revival of the teaching of judgment and eternal punishment. And yet only the Holy Spirit can make this truth terrifying. If He does not come alongside when such is preached, people will be unaffected.

Some people say, "If there were no heaven and no hell, I would still be a Christian." I know what they mean by that. But Paul vehemently disagrees. He would say that kind of thinking is sheer nonsense. "If in Christ we have hope in this life only, we are of all people most to be pitied" (1 Cor. 15:19, ESV). Paul had so much suffering from the day he was saved that he would have no reason for living if there were not a heaven to come. This is the most wonderful news: we are on our way to heaven. This is why Jesus died (John 3:16).

When the Holy Spirit convicts us as Jesus promised He would, we become convinced of what ultimately matters—and learn, therefore, the real reason people need to be saved.

For further study: Matthew 3:1–10; John 3:3–16; Romans 1:16–20; 2 Corinthians 5:10–21

Holy Spirit of glory and grace, thank You for showing us the gospel—why He was sent into this world, why He died, and how we may be saved. Deliver us from shallow thinking about the real reason Jesus died and why people need to be saved. In Jesus's name, amen.

_____

_____

_____

_____

_____

_____

_____

_____

_____

_____

Day 28

THE HOLY SPIRIT IS OUR GUIDE

H E WILL GUIDE you into all the truth" (John 16:13). Unless you are led to see truth by the Spirit, you will never see it. "The man without the Spirit does not accept the things that come from the Spirit of God, for they are foolishness to him, and he cannot understand them, because they are spiritually discerned" (1 Cor. 2:14). Without the Spirit we will likely think it is our great brain that keeps us from seeing what is there. Only by the Holy Spirit guiding us can we understand the Bible and then experience the joy of the Spirit.

My hobby for many years was bonefishing in the Florida Keys. A bonefish (called that because they are bony and virtually inedible) is a wily, skittish, hard-to-see, fast-as-lightning, shallow-water fish that is great fun to catch. They average in size around six to eight pounds. But if you have never tried it, you are unwise to do so the first time without a professional guide. When I first heard this, I refused to hire a guide. First, I didn't want to pay his fee. Second, I didn't want to admit I *needed* a guide. But after repeated failures on my own I gave in and hired a guide. The funny thing was, he took me to the exact spots in Largo Sound where I had fished for months without seeing any bonefish! With this kind of fishing—which requires stalking them and seeing them before they see you—it is imperative to see them before you cast to them. But I hadn't even seen the first one! But with the guide I saw them in no time! I will never forget it. I was eventually able to see them. And yet I would never have seen one on my own without a guide.

The Spirit "guides" us into truth—showing what is *there* but what cannot be seen without Him opening our eyes. It is humbling for prideful people to admit to the need of the Holy Spirit. The cost? Our pride being shattered. But once we are broken and enabled to see our stubbornness, the Spirit will show us amazing things in Scripture.

As it happens, I was recently in Bimini, Bahamas, to do some bonefishing. I hired a wonderful guide "Bonefish Tommy." Despite knowing how to see them (in the past), I realize how much I had forgotten on how to spot them, even in crystal-clear water only a foot or so deep. As a matter of fact, most of the fish I caught I had not seen at all; Tommy would usually tell me where to cast—and I would then catch them. I felt so dumb!

Sometimes we experienced Christians—who know

sound theology—need to humble ourselves and admit our need for further illumination by the Spirit. I need the Holy Spirit more than ever. I have been reading the Bible for some seventy years. I have read it through about forty times. But sometimes I feel I've barely begun to know God and His Word. We never outgrow our need for the Heavenly Guide to lead us to truth we have never seen before—but which has always been there.

Don't forget the most important thing according to Jesus: the Holy Spirit guides us into all *truth*. The truth referred to here is objective truth—not someone's subjective opinion. This means that if the Holy Spirit guides me and the Holy Spirit guides you, we will come to the same doctrinal position. There is one faith—the faith once for all delivered to the saints (Jude 3). For example, we will be in agreement that Jesus of Nazareth is the Messiah who was prophesied in the Old Testament. We will believe that He was the eternal *Logos* who was with God and was God and "sent" into this world. He was born of a virgin. He lived without sin. His death on the cross was for our sins. He was raised from the dead. He sent the Holy Spirit to do everything that was promised of Him. What is more, He is coming again!

This is objective truth. It is what the Holy Spirit will lead every believer to embrace. That is what is meant by the Holy Spirit being our guide. We have

His guidance on other things too. "In all your ways acknowledge him, and he will make your paths straight" (Prov. 3:6). But the main thing Jesus had in mind regarding the Holy Spirit being our guide is that He guides us into the truth. We will never be deceived if we listen to and follow Him.

For further study: Psalm 119:30–48; Isaiah 58:11; Galatians 1:6–9; 1 John 4:1–6

> *Holy Spirit of truth, I thank You that You will never mislead me or deceive me. I am thankful that it is impossible for You to lie. I ask You to correct me where I have gotten it wrong. Save me from defensiveness lest I miss the mark. Indeed, do lead me into all truth. In Jesus's name, amen.*

Day 29

THE HOLY SPIRIT SPEAKS ONLY WHAT THE FATHER GIVES HIM TO SAY

Y OU MAY RECALL that in our first segment (Day 1: "The Holy Spirit Is God") I mentioned that there are hymns and songs that address and praise the Holy Spirit. These make some Christians uneasy, all because of a faulty translation of John 16:13 in what is probably the best-known translation of the Bible. In many ways I still prefer the King James. But no translation is perfect.

These words of Jesus, referring to the Holy Spirit are: "He will not speak on his own; he will speak only what he hears" (John 16:13). The King James Version is sadly famous for translating this verse, "he shall not speak of himself," which is one of the more unfortunate translations in biblical translation history. I observed that it has led good people to infer that they should barely (if at all) mention the Holy Spirit lest they say what the Spirit Himself would never allow. This is a mistake. After all, the Holy Spirit wrote the

New Testament! This is how we know about the Holy Spirit!

The correct translation of John 16:13 is *not* that the Holy Spirit would not speak of Himself but that He will not speak "on his own," or "on his own authority" (ESV). This means He passes on only what the Father tells Him to say. That is what the verse means. Never be afraid to talk about the Holy Spirit. It is exactly what the Father and Son want you to do.

The Holy Spirit, in fact, had the exact same relationship with the Father that Jesus had. Jesus said, "I tell you the truth, the Son can do nothing by himself; he can do only what he sees his Father doing, because whatever the Father does the Son also does" (John 5:19). This means Jesus took His cue from the Father—what to say, where to go, when to heal, when to reply. He did *nothing* without receiving the green light from the Father. Therefore everything Jesus ever did had been orchestrated in heaven by the Father. The Son did nothing on His own. Ever.

That is exactly what the Holy Spirit is saying about Himself. The Spirit does nothing without the green light from the throne of grace—what to say, where to go, when to heal, when to reply. Concerning where to go, the disciples were once "kept by the Holy Spirit ["forbidden," KJV] from preaching the word in the province of Asia" (Acts 16:6). The Holy Spirit was doing what the Father ordered; for some reason it was the will of the Father that they not go there (at least then). The Holy Spirit did not retort, "I want to go to Asia." That was unthinkable. The disciples might have had thoughts like that. But not the Holy Spirit. The persons of the Trinity are utterly and eternally united. Luke continues: "When they [the disciples] came to the border of Mysia, they tried to enter Bithynia, but the Spirit of Jesus would not allow them to" (v. 7). God the Father orchestrated from heaven all that the Holy Spirit would say or do here on planet earth. That is the meaning of these words in John 16:13. Jesus never said that the Holy Spirit would not speak of Himself. In fact, He *does* speak of Himself.

First, since the entire New Testament is as inspired as the Old Testament, and we know the latter was written by the Holy Spirit, it follows that the Holy Spirit wrote the New Testament. If the Holy Spirit would not speak of Himself, we would have few if any references to the Spirit in the New Testament! Second, consider how much the Holy Spirit is mentioned in the Book of Acts, beginning with the account of what happened on the Day of Pentecost in Acts 2. Later, when Peter replied to the Sanhedrin, he said, "We are witnesses of these things, and *so is the Holy Spirit*" (Acts 5:32, emphasis added). Peter was undoubtedly *full* of the Spirit when he said that, and he gives specific mention to the Holy Spirit.

These things said, our preeminent and ultimate

focus should always be our Lord and Savior. The gospel is central: why God sent His Son, why He died, and why He was raised. Never lose sight of the major focus—Jesus Christ. That lost people go to hell. That saved people—those whose hope of heaven is only the blood Jesus shed—go to heaven. That is always the main thing. But let no one be inhibited when it comes to mentioning the Spirit. After all, this book you are reading is unashamedly about increasing our knowledge *of* the Spirit but also knowing *Him*, enjoying *Him*, and having intimacy with *Him*. This comes by the immediate and direct witness of the Holy Spirit.

Finally, don't forget the essential point Jesus is making about the Spirit. Jesus and the Holy Spirit have in common that they do not do or say *anything* without the direction from the Father. It was the way Jesus ministered on this planet and the way the Holy Spirit functions now.

For further study: Exodus 13:19; John 3:8; Acts 8:26–39; 13:2–4

> *Blessed Holy Spirit, I am so comforted by the knowledge that You do what the Father tells You to say and do—just as Jesus did. I love knowing that when I am led by the Holy Spirit, I am simultaneously being led by the Father. I only pray, let me miss*

nothing You would say to me. In Jesus's name, amen.

_____

_____

_____

_____

_____

_____

_____

_____

_____

_____

_____

_____

Day 30

THE HOLY SPIRIT WILL PREDICT THE FUTURE

THE HOLY SPIRIT is not only omnipresent but also omniscient. This means that He cannot learn. But don't feel sorry for Him. It is because He already knows everything. This includes knowledge of the future. Open theism (a deadly teaching) says God does not know the future but learns from us and needs our counsel what to do next.

In my book *Holy Fire* I relate an incident that happened to me in Carlisle, Ohio, in 1962. Seven years earlier—when I was still in Nashville—I had an open vision of being in a church that had theater-like seats instead of pews but with windows only on one side of the auditorium. I had no idea where this church was. I noticed that in the vision my father was present and was wearing a mint green suit (which was rather odd), and he came walking down the center aisle all the way to the front. He then turned and went back the same direction. That was it. I had no idea what it could mean. When I first preached in that church in the spring of 1962, I noticed the building had windows on one side; the church had theater-like seats with an aisle in the center. We later moved to Carlisle from Florida and began a ministry there on July 1, 1962. When my father phoned several days later to say he wanted to come and hear me preach the following Sunday, I told Louise what he would be wearing. Surprise, surprise; he wore the very suit I saw in the vision. When the service was over, I saw my father walking down the center aisle to the front. He then turned and went back in the same direction. That was it—exactly as it happened in the vision. It was as though I had seen a film of the incident seven years before.

What was the purpose? First, I am sure the reason was that I might know I was in God's will. My time in Carlisle was extremely hard. It was traumatic. But I never doubted that God wanted me there. The fulfillment of the vision was so comforting. And second, the vision proves that God knows the future—perfectly.

"He will tell you what is yet to come," said Jesus (John 16:13). That God knows the future is the basis for prophecy. In this book we have seen several references to the Holy Spirit in the Old Testament. *All* prophecies in the Old Testament—from Moses to Elijah and from Samuel to Malachi—were borne by the Holy Spirit. I wrote a book based on Isaiah 53, called *Why Jesus Died*.[1] Isaiah 53 is written in such a manner that one is amazed that Jews today could read that chapter and not see how Jesus and His death were perfectly predicted and fulfilled. "I make known the end from the beginning, from ancient times, what is still to come. I say: My purpose will stand, and I will do all that I please" (Isa. 46:10).

This is how Agabus knew a famine would be coming (Acts 11:28). This is how Paul knew the ship he was on would be shipwrecked (Acts 27:23–26). God also knows the present perfectly. This is how the Holy Spirit could convey to Ananias that the notorious Saul of Tarsus had just been converted (Acts 9:10–16).

Never forget: God knows the end from the beginning. He knows the future as perfectly as He knows the past.

One of the great "proofs of God" (should someone need them) and evidences for the infallibility of the Bible is the fact of prophecy being fulfilled. There could be no prophecy if God did not know the future—perfectly. When someone is given a true prophetic word, it is because they are carried up into the Spirit in a special manner, only because He knows the past, present, and future perfectly.

Some people ask, "How could the prophet Nathan in one stroke pronounce that David's sin of adultery and murder had been forgiven when the Law would not allow this?" "The LORD has taken away your sin," said Nathan (2 Sam. 12:13). And yet Nathan's word went right against the Mosaic Law that demanded death by stoning for either adultery or murder. David had committed both sins. And yet God forgave him immediately, according to Nathan. It was because Nathan had been carried up into the Spirit, who saw that the death of Jesus Christ removes *all sin*— including sin with a high hand. The Law had no provision for sin with a high hand. Nathan by the Holy Spirit brought this truth forward to apply to David. This, in fact, is how anybody in the Old Testament was saved. It is the future brought forward. Indeed, healing is the *eschaton*—the Last Day when we are glorified—brought forward. God knows the end from the beginning.

If one predicts what is to come, it is only because the Holy Spirit brings the future forward (so to speak) so that it can be seen in advance. Sometimes it is a clear vision (as mine was) that will be fulfilled literally. Sometimes a prophecy can be given symbolically, that one is given to see what is in the future but not literally. Isaiah 53 is written in such a manner that it could only be fully understood after the event unfolded.

In any case, the Holy Spirit can show "what is yet to come" when He is pleased to do so.

For further study: Deuteronomy 18:15 and Acts 3:22; Isaiah 53:7 and Luke 23:9; Micah 5:2 and Matthew 2:5; Zechariah 9:9 and Matthew 21:4–5

> *O omniscient Holy Spirit, I am thankful that You live in me. I am so glad that You know the future perfectly and that I am in Your hands. Show me all that You want me to know, even things that are yet to come, if You will. In Jesus's name, amen.*

_____

_____

_____

_____

_____

_____

_____

_____

_____

Day 31

THE HOLY SPIRIT WILL GLORIFY JESUS CHRIST

I SAID PREVIOUSLY THAT the gospel is central to all that we believe. The main thing is to keep the main thing the main thing; namely, that all who believe on the Son have eternal life; all others perish (which means they go to hell). When Jesus continued explain the role of the "one who comes alongside," He showed the Spirit's main focus: the second person of the Trinity—Jesus Christ.

"He will bring glory to me by taking from what is mine and making it known to you" (John 16:14). One of the interesting characteristics of the Trinity is that the persons of the Godhead heap praise on each other. As I said, there is no jealousy or rivalry in the Godhead. This is hard for some to grasp. The Father does not mind if you pray to Jesus or the Holy Spirit. The Father honors the Spirit and the Son. The Son honors the Father and the Spirit. The Spirit glorifies Christ and speaks only what He hears from the Father.

Glorifying Christ is honoring Him for:

1. Who He is

2. What He said

3. What He did for us

4. What He continues to do for us

5. What He will do

It is giving Jesus the honor *now* that He will receive openly on the Last Day—when every knee shall bow and every tongue confess that Jesus Christ is Lord to the glory of God the Father (Phil. 2:9–11). *You cannot praise Jesus too much. It is impossible to heap too much praise on the Lord Jesus Christ.* The Holy Spirit leads us to praise the Lord Jesus as He deserves, although we all wish we could do better. This is why Charles Wesley wrote, "O for a thousand tongues to sing my great Redeemer's praise."[1]

Jesus said that the Holy Spirit would "take what is mine." What is *His* and what is made known to us? Answer: (1) His work as Redeemer, and (2) the glory and praise Jesus Christ deserves—what belongs to Him. Jesus is the focus. He is the One who was *to be* glorified—and who *was* glorified. Jesus had prayed, "Father, the time has come. Glorify your Son, that your Son may glorify you…Glorify me in your presence with the glory I had with you before the world began" (John 17:1, 5). The glory of Christ is the focus. He is our Redeemer. He is the God-man. It is *not the Spirit* who is to be focused on when it comes to praise, honor, and glory. You may ask, "Is not the Holy Spirit God?" Yes. But it is not the Holy Spirit who indwelt a human body without measure. It is not the Holy Spirit who fulfilled the Law. It is not the Holy Spirit who lived without sin in a human body. It is not the Holy Spirit who died, who was raised from the dead, and who ascended to the right hand of God. It is not the Holy Spirit to whom every knee shall bow one day. So when Jesus said that the Holy Spirit would take what is "mine," He was stating that the focus would be on the Redeemer and Savior of the world, who would be glorified and made known to us.

"He will testify about me," Jesus also said (John 15:26). Jesus promised to make Himself as real to the disciples in the Spirit as He had been in the flesh. "In a little while [in a few days from then, in fact] you will see me no more [when He ascended to heaven]." But Jesus added, "And then after a little while [on the Day of Pentecost] you will see me" (John 16:16). How did they see Jesus? By the Holy Spirit. This is why Peter in his sermon that day quoted David, "I saw the Lord always before me" (Acts 2:25; Ps. 16:8). The disciples saw the Lord—in a vision that was absolutely real—as if He were physically present with them. When the Holy Spirit testified of Jesus, He made Jesus absolutely real to them. This was repeated in Acts 4:33, when "much grace" enabled them to testify of Jesus's resurrection. In other words, the Holy Spirit made the resurrection of Jesus absolutely real to them, as if before their very eyes. This is what Peter meant when he later said, "We are witnesses of these things, *and so is the Holy Spirit*" (Acts 5:32, emphasis added).

The Holy Spirit glorifying Jesus means the Spirit testifies that Jesus is the God-man (John 1:14). He also witnesses to the fact that one day all men and women who ever lived—the righteous and the wicked, the rich and the poor, kings and ordinary people— will get down on their knees and *proclaim* that Jesus Christ is Lord—God—to the glory of God the Father (Phil. 2:10–11). Not because they want to, but because they have to. All people will do this one day. You and I do it now!

For further study: John 14:25–31; 16:17–21; Acts 2:23–36; Romans 14:11; Philippians 2:5–11

> *O Holy Spirit, make me to see how real Jesus is—who died and was raised, who ascended to heaven and is coming again, and who will be worshipped by the whole earth on the Final Day. Grant that I myself will give Jesus the worship He deserves not only then but now. In Jesus's name, amen.*

_____

_____

_____

_____

_____

_____

_____

_____

_____

_____

_____

_____

_____

_____

_____

Day 32

THE HOLY SPIRIT CAN
BE BLASPHEMED

THE BLASPHEMY AGAINST the Spirit will not be forgiven" (Matt. 12:31). This is arguably the scariest passage in the New Testament. It is called the unpardonable sin because there is no forgiveness if one blasphemes the Holy Spirit. Many pastors have someone in their church who fears he or she may have committed this sin. I get messages from time to time on Twitter from people who fear they have blasphemed the Holy Spirit. It is usually from someone who has battled with sexual temptation and gave in.

What is the blasphemy of the Holy Spirit? First, it is not any sin against the moral law (Ten Commandments). It is not greed, stealing, or bearing false witness; it is not committing murder or adultery. King David committed both murder and adultery, and he was forgiven. The unpardonable sin is committed when one's *final verdict* regarding the gospel is to show contempt for the Spirit's testimony—which is to glorify Christ. It is one's final decision to undermine the Holy Spirit's witness that Jesus is God in the flesh. One therefore blasphemes the Holy Spirit by finally denying that Jesus is God in the flesh—or saying that Jesus has an evil spirit. In Mark's account it is written: "Whoever blasphemes against the Holy Spirit will never be forgiven; he is guilty of an eternal sin". And then Mark added that Jesus said this because they were saying, "He [Jesus] has an evil spirit" (Mark 3:29–30). How can you know you have not committed the unpardonable sin? If you can testify from your heart that Jesus is God, worry no more.

I watched a conference on YouTube in which the speakers poked fun at certain people who were falling out under the power of the Spirit and laughing their heads off. Ironically some of these speakers were laughing as they watched videos of people who were laughing their heads off. One of the speakers had also had written that speaking in tongues is voodoo. This is perilously close to saying the Holy Spirit is evil. I don't think this man would mean to say that. But it was sobering to watch these men who were laughing at sincere Christians and to read what I just referred to. I choose to come short of saying these men who were mocking blasphemed the Spirit. But it is scary what they were doing.

In my old church in Ashland, Kentucky, we had evangelists come in two or three times a year to hold *revivals*—missions, usually lasting two weeks each.

It was common for the minister to preach on blaspheming the Holy Spirit at least once—usually on the last evening—scaring everybody nearly to death. However, I cannot recall ever hearing a minister explain exactly what the unpardonable sin was—or how it could be committed. I fear it was used sometimes as a ploy to get people to run to the altar, lest they commit this sin and inevitably go to hell.

And yet I have had people in Westminster Chapel come to see me, worrying that they had blasphemed the Spirit. One dear man—who was solid in his faith—remembers a time before he was converted that he said, "Damn you, Holy Ghost." After he was converted, he read the accounts about the blasphemy of the Spirit. Although he was serving the Lord faithfully, this incident haunted him. When I showed him that blaspheming the Spirit is showing contempt for the *testimony* of the Spirit, pointing to the person of Jesus, he was set free and never troubled again. I repeat: if you can say from your *heart* that Jesus Christ is God, you have not committed this sin. Paul said that no person can say "Jesus is Lord" but by the Holy Spirit (1 Cor. 12:3).

Did Ananias and Sapphira blaspheme the Holy Spirit since Peter said they lied to the Spirit and they were instantly struck dead? No. They were believers who were overtaken with greed. This can happen to any of us. There is no hint they questioned the person of Jesus. They were struck dead because they willfully lied about money in the immediate and direct presence of the Holy Spirit. God made an example of them to show the responsibility we have when God is present like that. If the Holy Spirit were to return to the church at that level of power—as I myself expect will come one day—we can expect this sort of thing to happen again.

If you can say in your heart of hearts, "Jesus is Lord," it is because you have the Holy Spirit. You have not blasphemed Him.

For further study: Matthew 12:30–32; Mark 3:23–30; 1 Corinthians 12:1–3; 1 John 5:16–17

> *Gracious Holy Spirit, I thank You with my whole heart that I can affirm from my heart what You testify about Jesus. I thank You that I can also testify that Jesus was born of a virgin, conceived by You, and that He was and is the Son of God and God in the flesh. In Jesus's name, amen.*

Day 33

THE HOLY SPIRIT IS
OUR REMINDER

D O YOU HAVE a bad memory? Do you ever read a book and say to yourself, "I wish I could remember this point"? Do you ever hear a sermon and wish, "If only I could remember this"?

Consider the disciples of Jesus. They heard almost everything He said publicly for three years. They heard the Sermon on the Mount. They heard the parables. They heard His dialogues with the Pharisees and Sadducees. They may have thought, "If only I could remember all these wonderful teachings."

Not to worry. Jesus told them that the Holy Spirit will "remind you of everything I have said to you" (John 14:26). He will "bring to your remembrance all that I have said to you" (ESV). If you fear you have forgotten what you heard, don't worry! The Holy Spirit will remind you of what you were taught.

This is so relevant today. People ask, "Why should I read my Bible? I don't understand it. Why should I memorize Scripture? Why should I listen to teaching— it is often so boring."

I reply: Even if you don't understand it and think you won't remember it, you are taking in more than you consciously realize at the time. In an appropriate moment—possibly at a time you least expect—the Spirit will remind you of what you heard.

There are two things we need to realize in this connection. First, the Holy Spirit promises to remind you of what you *heard—read or learned.* In other words, He will remind you of *what is there.* If there is nothing there to be reminded of, how can the Holy Spirit bring it back to your remembrance? What if you are empty-headed when it comes to Bible knowledge? If you don't take the time to read your Bible, how can the Holy Spirit remind you of what you have not read? This is why we all need a Bible reading plan that will take you through the entire Bible in a year. This is why you need good teaching, good preaching. As for memorizing Scripture, it is sadly extremely rare these days. I am so thankful I was required to memorize Scripture as I was growing up.

You may say, "I need the Holy Spirit to fall on me. I need the power of God to make me fall on the floor." I reply: if you are empty-headed when you fall, you will be empty-headed when you get up! The Holy Spirit promises to remind you of *what is there.* I will repeat: if there is nothing there to be reminded of, whatever do you expect the Holy Spirit to do?

I believe a great move of the Holy Spirit is coming.

I also believe it is coming soon. I believe it will be the greatest outpouring of the Holy Spirit since the Day of Pentecost. Those who know their Bibles will be the likely candidates to be sovereignly used of God. If so, how would *you* like to be right in the middle of it? I have a conviction that only those who take oil in their lamps—like the wise virgins in Jesus's parable of the ten virgins—will enjoy this outpouring of the Spirit. Oil refers to the Spirit. The lamps refer to the Word. "Your word is a lamp to my feet and a light for my path" (Ps. 119:105). In other words, the Word and Spirit together.

The second thing we need to realize is this. Jesus's word about the Holy Spirit reminding us of what we learned assumes that the Spirit is in us ungrieved, that the Dove has come down on us and remained. It is when the Holy Spirit is ungrieved and unquenched that we will remember what we have learned. But if I am angry, bitter, holding grudges, and having a life-style of pointing the finger, the Dove lifts and leaves me to myself. Not absolutely, because the Spirit is with us forever. But the sense of His presence lifts—the anointing that makes things flow easily.

Indeed, what Jesus promised about the Holy Spirit assumes that the Spirit is unquenched and ungrieved in us. This is why Jesus was so real to the disciples on the Day of Pentecost and also during the days immediately following that glorious day. We need not expect

Jesus to be real to us or be reminded of things we previously learned when we are in an agitated and bitter condition. But when we have totally forgiven those who have hurt us, have mistreated us, have lied to us, and have been grossly unfair, the Dove comes down. Jesus is real. The Bible comes alive. And we find ourselves remembering things we had forgotten—sometimes the most obscure verses in the Bible and even those boring sermons we managed to sit through!

For further study: Luke 22:14–23; Acts 11:15–17; 1 Corinthians 11:23–26; 2 Peter 1:12–15

> *Blessed Holy Spirit, grant me to know afresh that I have totally forgiven all those who have hurt me in any way; Your anointing is more important than my getting vengeance. Please grant that You will come to me ungrieved so that I will have memory of all I need for this day. In Jesus's name, amen.*

_____

_____

_____

_____

Day 34

THE HOLY SPIRIT GIVES POWER

IN THIS BOOK we have seen that God is omnipresent (present everywhere) and omniscient (all knowing). The Holy Spirit is also omnipotent—all powerful. After all, when you consider that the Holy Spirit was involved in Creation, that is proof of His power. It was the Holy Spirit who divided the Red Sea when the Israelites crossed it. It was the Holy Spirit who caused fire to fall on Mount Carmel. It was the Holy Spirit who enabled Elijah and Elisha to raise people from the dead. It was the Holy Spirit who converted three thousand people on the Day of Pentecost. It was the Holy Spirit who caused the place to be shaken when the disciples prayed (Acts 4:31).

Moments before Jesus ascended to heaven, He said (probably His final words on this earth), "You will receive power when the Holy Spirit comes on you; and you will be my witnesses in Jerusalem, and in all Judea and Samaria, and to the ends of the earth" (Acts 1:8). I don't think this promise about the Spirit interested the disciples as much as it should have. They had something else on their minds. They really wanted to know if Jesus would at long last be restoring the kingdom to Israel (v. 6). Jesus evaded the question and promised them power that would come when the Spirit came on them. This promise was fulfilled on the Day of Pentecost.

The power of the Holy Spirit was experienced basically in three areas. First, there came a demonstration of supernatural power—that which defied a natural explanation. Mind you, not a high level of faith was needed for what they heard, saw, and felt. It was heard by their ears, seen with their eyes, and felt in their bodies. Although Jesus said the kingdom of God would not be visible (meaning an earthly government), ironically the initial evidences of the Holy Spirit were physical! The first sensation was hearing. Suddenly there came from heaven a *sound* like a "mighty rushing wind." The 120 disciples sitting (not standing, not kneeling) inside the house were given power to hear and see and feel what was unprecedented in Israel's history. They looked at each other and saw "tongues as of fire" resting upon each one's head! It was a visible display of holy fire. This came with their being "filled with the Holy Spirit." They began to speak "in other tongues as the Spirit gave them utterance" (Acts 2:1–4, esv). Although Mark 16:17 [a passage in dispute by some scholars since it was not apparently in the earliest manuscripts we have] indicated that Jesus's followers would speak "in new tongues," I don't believe the 120 disciples were prepared for this. They were enabled to do this as the Spirit gave them "utterance." They didn't work it up. The tongues on the Day of Pentecost were recognizable languages. The multitude that had gathered heard each one speaking "in his own language" (Acts 2:6).

Second, they were given inner power to grasp what had previously been dark or mysterious. It was not until the Holy Spirit came on them that the disciples came to see the real purpose of Jesus coming to the earth. They now understood that (1) the falling of the Spirit was a fulfillment of Joel (Joel 2:28–32); (2) Jesus's death on the cross was no accident but was purposed for our salvation; (3) His resurrection demonstrated who Jesus was—that He was the Son of God; (4) Jesus was now at the right hand of God; (5) that the ascension took place to make way for the Holy Spirit; (6) people needed to be forgiven of their sins; and (7) all those who heard Peter's sermon could be forgiven and could receive the Holy Spirit if they repented and were baptized (Acts 2:14–39). It all fell in place for Peter and those who had been filled with the Spirit.

Third, this power meant power to witness. Acts 1:8 connects two things, making them virtually inseparable—power and witnessing. The power was not merely for their enjoyment—although it must have been thrilling for them all. It is what enabled Peter to confront thousands of Jews with utter fearlessness. The same Peter who cowardly denied knowing Jesus to a Galilean servant girl only seven weeks before was now telling the powerful Jews of the day what *they* needed to do. In fact, Peter's preaching was so effective that the hearers were "cut to the heart"—something that only the Holy Spirit can do—and asked, "What shall we do?" (Acts 2:37). They were scoffing at first, dismissing the 120 who were filled with the Spirit as having "too much wine" (v. 13). I personally doubt that they were poking fun at them over the tongues—hearing what was said but understood in their own language would have sobered them. When we get to heaven and see a DVD of the entire episode, I predict we will see that many of these Spirit-filled disciples were laughing their heads off with extreme joy. But after hearing Peter, the scoffers were now begging to know what to do next! The explanation: power, a supernatural energy that defies a natural explanation.

Paul said that the kingdom of God consists not in talk but in "power" (1 Cor. 4:20). I have no doubt that the power of the Holy Spirit is relevant and available not only for insight and witnessing but also for holy living and other demonstrations of the supernatural.

For further study: Luke 24:45–49; Acts 2:37–41; 3:6–16; 13:8–12

> *Omnipotent Holy Spirit, please hasten the day when our own generation might see Your mighty power. Forgive me for having so little of Your power. Please apply Jesus's blood to me for my cleansing and being used. Grant that I may have an increased power to witness and to see many saved. In Jesus's name, amen.*

_____

_____

_____

_____

_____

_____

_____

_____

Day 35

THE HOLY SPIRIT MANIFESTS THROUGH VARIOUS SPIRITUAL GIFTS

YOU WILL RECALL that cessationism is the unbiblical theory that the gifts of the Holy Spirit "ceased" at some point in the early church. I don't mean to be unfair, but I believe many conservative evangelicals are quick to embrace the teaching of cessationism not because of the gifts of the Spirit generally but the gift of speaking in tongues particularly. I doubt that many today would uphold cessationism were it not for the gift of tongues. That is where the offense is. It is the only gift that challenges your pride. Nobody whom I know of objects to gifts such as the gift of wisdom or healing. Some may well object to the prophetic gift or word of knowledge— but only because these have been so abused. The real offense is tongues.

"Now to each one the manifestation of the Spirit is given for the common good," these including: wisdom, words of knowledge, faith, healing, miraculous powers, prophecy, discernment of spirits, different kinds of tongues, and interpretation of tongues (1 Cor. 12:7–10). There are further gifts listed, such as the ability to "help others" and "gifts of administration" (v. 28). There are (what some call) motivational gifts in Romans 12:3–8. A recondite issue among some Christians—including Pentecostals and charismatics—is whether the evidence of the baptism of the Holy Spirit is always and necessarily speaking in tongues. Is the gift of tongues or praying in tongues (1 Cor. 14:2, 14) the same phenomenon as the one that the 120 received on the Day of Pentecost (Acts 2:4)? Possibly not. It may have been something different. The best scholars among Pentecostals and charismatics differ on this, and I see no need to make an issue here.

I have a chapter on spiritual gifts in *Holy Fire* in which the gifts are explained in somewhat more detail than below. Paul said we should all earnestly desire the greater gifts. He puts wisdom as first on the list. Perhaps he did so because he considers wisdom the most important. But surely the gifts of healing and of doing miracles would also be among the greater gifts. To those who point out that the gift of tongues is at the bottom of the list, and therefore the least important, I have an answer: if you really want the greater gifts, be willing to start at the bottom! They who humble themselves will be exalted. It can be embarrassing and humbling to speak in tongues. That would show how much you "earnestly desire" the gifts of the Spirit. I will briefly mention each of those described in 1 Corinthians 12:8–10:

Wisdom. This is the presence of the mind of the Spirit, enabling you to know the next step forward in what you should say or do. Wisdom consists not in more education or a high IQ but having the right word at the right time whether it be for yourself or others. Sadly it is the last gift so many seem to want and yet is the most needed.

Message of knowledge. Better known these days as "word [Gr. *logos*] of knowledge," this gift *could* refer to theological and biblical knowledge, but it may also be understood as being a "special word" that a person needs urgently: a timely and relevant message from the Spirit that assures one that God and not man has spoken.

Faith. This is not saving or justifying faith but rather an amazing ability to trust God in a crisis. It is when you are amazed at your ability to cope when all things have gone wrong. It could be a permanent gift or something given for a needed moment.

Healing. This gift shows that Jesus's ministry of healing did not end when He ascended to God's right hand. God intended that healing the sick should continue until Jesus comes. What happened in the Book of Acts can happen today. Some people seem to have a special gift in this area.

Miraculous powers. It is not easy to determine the difference between healing of the sick and miracles (the Greek words are used interchangeably). However, it is possible that healing can be gradual and miracles may take place instantly. The forty-year-old lame man who never walked was suddenly enabled to walk—and leap—at the Gate Beautiful (although this miracle is called healing; Acts 3:1–16). This gift of miracles may also refer to casting out demons.

Prophecy. This is not a gift like Isaiah's, but it is more like Agabus's prophecies, as we have seen. There are levels of prophetic gifts. God *could* raise up an Elijah, and perhaps has, but the gift of prophecy Paul seems to be urging (1 Cor. 14:1) is mostly for the edification of the body of Christ.

Distinguishing between spirits. This important gift enables one to recognize the demonic but also the genuine Holy Spirit. Nothing is said here of casting out demons; the gift of the miraculous would apply to this. But never underestimate the importance of a person having the ability to recognize the Holy Spirit Himself in a day when there is so much of the counterfeit.

Speaking in different kinds of tongues. This is popularly known as a "prayer language," and yet Paul here mentions "different kinds" of tongues, implying that one may not always speak in the same language each time—whether it is a known language on earth or an angelic tongue. Or it may mean one person speaks in one language and another person in an entirely different one.

Interpretation of tongues. Paul does not say *translation* but *interpretation*. It does not require a word-for-word translation but conveying the spirit of one's message in tongues. If one speaks a tongue in the church, Paul required that someone interpret. I'm sure a lot of the counterfeit has been manifested here, but I have also seen the real, which can be beautiful.

It is debatable whether one has a gift permanently or as needed. In any case, the gifts are "irrevocable" (Rom. 11:29; "without repentance," KJV), a sober reminder that we should not fancy ourselves to be spiritual because we exercise any of these gifts.

For further study: Romans 12:3–12; 1 Corinthians 1:4–9; Ephesians 4:7–16; James 5:13–16

> *Blessed Holy Spirit, thank You for granting gifts to the body of Christ. Grant that I myself will truly desire earnestly the greater gifts. Let me want them so much that I will seek the less spectacular or the more humbling in order that I might glorify the name of Jesus. We pray in His name, amen.*

_____

_____

_____

_____

_____

_____

_____

_____

_____

_____

_____

_____

_____

_____

Day 36

THE HOLY SPIRIT DIRECTS PEOPLE TO JESUS AND MAKES HIM REAL

HAVE YOU CONSIDERED how essential the work of the Holy Spirit is in evangelism? When Jesus said to Nicodemus, "You must be born again," He immediately added something about the Holy Spirit: "The wind blows wherever it pleases. You hear its sound, but you cannot tell where it comes from or where it is going. So it is with everyone born of the Spirit" (John 3:7–8). Jesus is saying that every conversion is a work of sovereign grace of the Holy Spirit. As we were passive in our natural birth, so too are we when born of the Holy Spirit. It is what the Holy Spirit does.

Does this surprise you? James said, "Of his own will he brought us forth by the word of truth, that we should be a kind of firstfruits of his creatures" (James 1:18, ESV). This means no conversion is an accident. Our natural birth was not an accident. God gives each of us life and breath. "From one man he made every nation of men, that they should inhabit the whole earth; and he determined the times set for them and the exact places where they should live" (Acts 17:26). God chose when and where we should be born. Why? "That men would seek him and perhaps reach out for him and find him" (v. 27). We are born "dead" in transgressions and sins, "but because of his great love for us, God, who is rich in mercy, made us alive with Christ even when we were dead in transgressions—it is by grace you have been saved" (Eph. 2:1, 4–5). This means we cannot take credit for being saved. "Where, then, is boasting?" asks Paul, who then answers: "It is excluded" (Rom. 3:27). Conversion is what the Holy Spirit does. It is not of works lest we boast (Eph. 2:9).

We saw earlier that Jesus said of the Holy Spirit, "He will testify about me" (John 15:26). What makes people want to turn to Jesus? The Holy Spirit. What makes Jesus real? The Holy Spirit. What makes what He did for us—dying on the cross and being raised from the dead—real? The Holy Spirit.

This is why Jesus said, "No one can come to me unless the Father who sent me draws them" (John 6:44). We are all born "dead"—"dead in your transgressions and sins" (Eph. 2:1). Can a dead man speak? Can a dead man hear? Can a dead man move? Can a dead man make a choice? Jesus's statement in John 6:44 came in the midst of what Bible teachers call *the hard teachings of Jesus*. At the beginning of this discourse Jesus had a following of five thousand (v. 10).

At the end, "Many of his disciples turned back and no longer followed him" (v. 66). Jesus elaborated on His various *hard* sayings: "The Spirit gives life; the flesh counts for nothing...This is why I told you that no one can come to me unless the Father has enabled him" (vv. 63, 65).

What is the aim of the Holy Spirit's witness? Jesus Christ. The Holy Spirit directs people to Jesus. "He will testify about me." It is the Spirit who makes people see *why* Jesus died and rose again. Remember that the Eleven (now that Judas Iscariot is out of the picture) did not know *why* Jesus died or rose from the dead even after they saw His resurrected body. It was not until the Holy Spirit fell on them on the Day of Pentecost that it all came together for them.

Charles Spurgeon once told how he himself was converted. He asked, "Why am I a Christian?" He concluded: it was because he heard the gospel. "But," he asked, "why did I believe it?" Then, like a flash, "I saw that God was at the bottom of it all"; he owed his salvation to sheer grace alone. Dr. Lloyd-Jones used to say that a Christian is a person who is surprised that he is a Christian!

I was invited to meet the late Margaret Thatcher when she was prime minister of Great Britain. I was given several minutes of private time with her just before I gave the invocation at a lawyer's convention in Royal Albert Hall. But lo and behold, who would be waiting to meet her, only to shake her hand? Chief Justice of the Supreme Court Warren Burger, Vice President Walter Mondale, and the American ambassador to St. James Court. Then it was announced that there would be a photograph of these dignitaries with the prime minister. At that point I stepped back to watch. "Come here, Dr. Kendall; you are to be in this photo," I was told. I walked over self-consciously to be included, to be photographed with these important people. I felt like a fraud. I did not deserve to be there for one second. But I was invited, and I accepted the invitation. When we get to heaven, we will all have this in common: we don't deserve to be there. But we were invited, and we accepted the invitation.

Martin Luther said he expects three surprises in heaven: (1) there will be those present he did not expect to be there, (2) there will be those missing he expected to be there, and (3) he is there himself!

For further study: Matthew 11:25–30; John 6:61–65; Romans 8:28–30; Ephesians 2:1–9

> *O sovereign Holy Spirit, I am so aware of my unworthiness before You. I so don't deserve to be Your child. Thank You for wooing me and giving me life. Save me from ever boasting that I am saved when I know it is all by Your grace. In Jesus's name, amen.*

_____

_____

_____

_____

_____

_____

_____

_____

_____

_____

_____

_____

_____

_____

Day 37

THE HOLY SPIRIT MANIFESTS
THROUGH VARIOUS FRUIT

T HE FRUIT OF the Spirit is love, joy, peace, patience, kindness, goodness, faithfulness, gentleness and self-control" (Gal. 5:22–23). I think it is possible for one to have the gifts of the Spirit without the fruit of the Spirit. I think too one can have the fruit of the Spirit without the gifts of the Spirit. Charismatics and Pentecostals tend to emphasize the gifts; conservative evangelicals and Reformed Christians tend to stress the fruits.

A brief synopsis of the Prologue in *Holy Fire* is perhaps in order: there has been a silent divorce in the church, speaking generally, between the Word and the Spirit. When there is a divorce, sometimes the children stay with the mother, sometimes with the father. In this divorce there are those on the Word side emphasizing sound doctrine, especially Romans, and those on the Spirit side emphasizing the Holy Spirit, especially the Book of Acts. Sadly it seems to be one or the other almost wherever I go in the world.

The need is for both. I believe the simultaneous combination will result in spontaneous combustion. The Word and Spirit coming together will bring about the next move of the Holy Spirit, in my opinion.

I will briefly mention each of the fruit of the Spirit as found in Galatians 5:22–23.

Love. This is the first fruit of the Spirit that Paul lists and is actually the sum total of all the fruit of the Holy Spirit. If indeed we fulfilled all that is described by Paul in 1 Corinthians 13, I am pretty sure we would experience all the fruit that follow— joy, peace, patience, and so forth. Paul means *agape* love (selfless love), not *philia* (brotherly love) or *eros* (physical love). Read 1 Corinthians 13, noting that "love is patient, love is kind. It does not envy, it does not boast, it is not proud. It is not rude, it is not self-seeking, it is not easily angered, it keeps no record of wrongs" (vv. 4–5). Why do we keep records? To prove we have paid. Why do we keep a record of wrongs? To remind another of their faults. Love tears up all records of wrong—whether it be your friend or enemy, your spouse or neighbor. Total forgiveness means that all the fruit of the Spirit follow.

Joy. This is an inward state when the absence of any condemnation allows you to experience the Lord's own joy. Happiness comes from outward things; joy is internal and comes by the ungrieved Spirit.

Peace. This something that Satan cannot produce.

The flesh cannot produce it. It is a fruit of the Spirit that witnesses to your eternal salvation and your pleasing the Lord.

Patience. This is a supernatural ability to *wait*, not merely to wait upon the Lord but also upon people! Instead of snapping your finger and expecting others to jump, you let them be themselves without your moralizing them.

Kindness. This means being nice. Considerate. Friendly. It is what makes people want to be around you. Does it surprise you that being nice to people is a fruit of the Holy Spirit?

Goodness. This is perhaps the hardest of the fruit of the Spirit to define. It is the combination of honesty and generosity. It can be used interchangeably with virtue. I think transparent integrity best defines goodness.

Faithfulness. God is faithful; He will never let us down. He keeps His word. If we are faithful, we will be consistent in keeping our word and demonstrating *agape* love.

Gentleness. This means the willingness to yield; it's the opposite of being harsh. It is being unruffled when your plans suddenly fall though. One thinks of the dove, a symbol of the Holy Spirit, as opposed to a pigeon, which is boisterous and a symbol of the counterfeit.

Self-control. This means having self-discipline regarding your temper, appetite, handling money, ambition, lifestyle, or coping with disappointment with ease.

Whereas the gifts of the Spirit are granted without repentance, the fruit emerge in proportion to our obedience. The gifts are sovereignly bestowed and irrevocable; they do not prove how spiritual a person is, whereas the fruit of the Spirit do indicate one's spirituality. As I said above, Word people, speaking generally, tend to focus on the fruit; Spirit people focus more on the gifts.

Why not both?

For further study: Romans 11:19; 1 Corinthians 13; Galatians 5:17–25; James 3:17–18

> *Gracious Holy Spirit, I am ashamed that I do not manifest Your fruit as I should, and I ask for Your forgiveness. I pray that my life will be one that shows Your power in spiritual gifts as well as graces that demonstrate Your fruit. In Jesus's name, amen.*

_____

_____

_____

_____

Day 38

THE HOLY SPIRIT USES THE LAYING ON OF HANDS

A T SOME STAGE in the life of the early church there emerged a practice by which the power of the Holy Spirit was transferred through the laying on of hands. This was actually done some thirteen hundred years before by Moses. The Lord said to Moses, "Take Joshua the son of Nun, a man in whom is the Spirit, and lay your hand on him" (Num. 27:18, ESV). Moses did precisely that. "He laid his hands on him and commissioned him" (v. 23, ESV). Note that Joshua already had the Spirit. But he needed more. There was both a renewal and a commissioning in the laying on of hands. Joshua was "filled with the spirit of wisdom *because* Moses had laid his hands on him" (Deut. 34:9, emphasis added).

A part of Jesus's ministry was that He laid hands on people or merely touched them for their benefit. He came to Peter's house and saw Peter's mother-in-law lying in bed with a fever. "He touched her hand and the fever left her" (Matt. 8:14–15). A ruler of the synagogue pleaded with Jesus, "My little daughter is dying. Please come and put your hands on her so that she will be healed and live" (Mark 5:23). Jesus came to her house, "took her by the hand and...the girl stood up and walked around...At this they were completely astonished" (vv. 41–42). Jesus healed a blind man by putting His "hands on the man's eyes. Then his eyes were opened, his sight was restored, and he saw everything clearly" (Mark 8:25).

Jesus also laid His hands on children (Matt. 19:15). Have you ever wondered how those children turned out? We will find out in heaven!

In Hebrews 6:1–2 The writer refers to six doctrines that he calls "elementary." One of these is "laying on of hands." What is the purpose? Two things. First, to transfer the anointing of the Holy Spirit. Second, to launch one into special ministry, or ordination. The first reference to the laying on of hands in the early church was when "signs and wonders were regularly done among the people by the hands of the apostles" (Acts 5:12, ESV). The second reference is when the first deacons were chosen in order to lighten the load of the apostles. After the seven men were chosen, the apostles prayed and "laid their hands on them" (Acts 6:6). In this case it is not clear whether the laying on of hands resulted in an increased anointing (probably) or if it was to show apostolic approval (certainly). Paul would later counsel Timothy not to be hasty in the "laying on of hands" lest the wrong person be given approval (1 Tim. 5:22). While the church fasted and prayed in Antioch, "the Holy Spirit said, 'Set apart for me Barnabas and Saul for the work to which I have called them.' So after they had fasted and prayed, they placed their hands on them and sent them off" (Acts 13:2–3). This occasion demonstrated both approval and increased power for these two men. Over the centuries the Christian church has maintained the laying on of hands with particular reference to ordination. And it is always hoped that a measure of the Holy Spirit was simultaneously transferred when this takes place.

Most occasions regarding the laying on of hands were not for ordination but for sheer transfer of power—sometimes for receiving the Spirit, other times for signs and wonders. Paul and Barnabas spoke boldly for the Lord, "who bore witness to the word of his grace, granting signs and wonders to be done by their hands" (Acts 14:3, ESV). When Paul was in Ephesus, it was the laying on of hands that resulted in the Ephesians being baptized with the Spirit and "speaking in tongues and prophesying" (Acts 19:6, ESV). God did "extraordinary miracles by the hands of Paul" (v. 11, ESV).

When the apostles heard that people in Samaria had accepted the word of God, they sent Peter and John to them. They prayed that the Samaritans might receive the Holy Spirit because the Spirit had not yet come upon any of them. "Then Peter and John placed their hands on them, and they received the Holy Spirit" (Acts 8:17). And yet Ananias, who was not an apostle, was used in the embryonic phase in the new life of Saul of Tarsus. Ananias, though very anxious about going to Saul (who was considered dangerous), did as he was told. "Placing his hands on Saul, he said, 'Brother Saul, the Lord—Jesus, who appeared to you on the road as you were coming here—has sent me so that you may see again and be filled with the Holy Spirit'" (Acts 9:17). Saul was filled with the Spirit and was instantly healed.

The laying on of hands was used in transferring anointing for healing. When Paul was in Malta, a man was sick with "fever and dysentery." Paul visited him and prayed, and "placed his hands on him and healed him" (Acts 28:8). James said that if there was a sick person, the elders should "pray over him and anoint him with oil in the name of the Lord" (James 5:14).

As I said above, we used both the anointing of oil and laying on of hands in our final years at Westminster Chapel. We saw some extraordinary healings, including exorcisms.

A lady came to me after I was preaching in Scotland. She asked me to pray for her headache. I put my hands on both of her temples and prayed briefly and simply, "In Jesus's name be healed," then went on my way. I would normally have forgotten this. But four months later the lady wrote to me to say that she had had a severe sinus condition for five years. That week was the worse she ever had, and on the day she asked me to pray for her, she had the most awful headache of her life. She said that when I prayed for her, she felt "nothing." But a few hours later she noticed that the headache was gone—and the sinus condition as well. This goes to show that the absence of an immediate manifestation should not discourage us.

My wife, Louise, and our son, TR, have had life-changing experiences through the laying on of hands. Louise was instantaneously healed. TR was brought back to the Lord. Why the laying on of hands? God's ways are higher than our ways. Don't try to figure Him out. Just accept that He uses things that seem foolish to most people!

For further study: Numbers 27:18–23; Acts 6:1–7; 9:10–19; James 5:13–16

> *Dear Holy Spirit, there are so many things in Your Word I don't understand. Give me grace not to question but to accept that Your ways and Your thoughts are higher than my ways. Grant me too the power to bless others through my own hands, unworthy though I am. In Jesus's name, amen.*

_____

_____

_____

_____

_____

_____

_____

_____

_____

_____

_____

_____

_____

Day 39

THE HOLY SPIRIT INTERCEDES FOR US

HAVE YOU EVER wondered whether or not you were truly praying in the will of God? Or have you wanted to be sure you were praying in the will of God? After all, God hears us only when we pray in His will (1 John 5:14). John adds, "If we *know that he hears us* [a big 'if']—whatever we ask—we know that we have what we asked of him" (v. 15). This kind of knowing is quite rare, in my opinion. At least my own experience suggests that it is rare. You may reply, "But if you were more spiritual, you would know all the time that you pray in the will of God." Really? What about the apostle Paul? Would you say he was a spiritual man? And yet he said:

> In the same way, the Spirit helps us in our weakness. We do not know what we ought to pray for, but the Spirit himself intercedes for us with groans that words cannot express. And he who searches our hearts knows the mind of

the Spirit, because the Spirit intercedes for the
saints in accordance with God's will.

—ROMANS 8:26–27

According to Paul, then, the Holy Spirit intercedes
for us when we don't know how to pray or what to
pray for, but the Spirit knows and intercedes in the
will of God. The problem is, you and I are not given
to know the content of the Holy Spirit's intercession.
If only we could have a direct line to the throne of
grace and eavesdrop on the Holy Spirit's actual prayer
(like in the old days when some of us had party lines
and could hear other people's conversations), then we
could know God's will in that moment! But like it or
not, we don't know what the Holy Spirit is praying.
We know He intercedes for us "with groans that
words cannot express" ("too deep for words," ESV).
The question is: *Who does the groaning*? Is it the
Holy Spirit? Is it us? Is it both? Could it be that we
groan as we pray but know the Spirit groans with us?
We can't always put words to our prayers. Sometimes
you can't articulate the thoughts. You just groan.
Inwardly plead. Yearn.

But there is a big plus in this inward dilemma: the
Holy Spirit moves in and prays for us. And when He
does, it is always according to the will of God!

When Paul says that Christ "also" makes intercession for us, does this mean that in *addition* to all He

has done for us that He *also* intercedes for us (v. 34)? Or does this mean that not only does the Holy Spirit intercede for us, but "also" Christ intercedes for us? Whatever, we know that both Jesus and the Holy Spirit intercede for us! These two intercessors have in common that their prayers for us are in the will of God.

When Paul said, "I live by the faith of the Son of God" (Gal. 2:20, KJV), part of the meaning is that Jesus prays for him with a perfect faith! Paul knows that his own faith is imperfect. But when he lives by the faith of the Son of God, Paul realizes that Jesus is always praying for him with perfect faith and in the will of God. And Paul depends on that.

If Paul lives by the faith of the Son of God, it follows also that we can live by the faith of the Holy Spirit. For when the Spirit intercedes for us, He does not say, "Please help my unbelief"! Hardly. When the Holy Spirit intercedes, He knows that His prayer will be answered because He only intercedes in the will of God. And I can live by that!

Question: Do the groanings that words cannot express refer to praying in tongues? Yes, in my honest opinion. I say that because: (1) Paul admits when he speaks or prays in tongues he has no idea what he is saying, that only God knows (1 Cor. 14:2); (2) Paul speaks of praying with the spirit (v. 15), which is what praying in tongues is, according to the context; and

(3) Paul added that he speaks in tongues more than anyone in Corinth (v. 18). It therefore makes perfect sense when Paul does not know what to pray for but prays with groanings that he would be praying in tongues at that time. After all, don't we all want to be sure we are praying in the will of God? I am not saying that those who do not pray in tongues do not get the benefit of Romans 8:26–27. God would hear our heartfelt sighs without praying in tongues. But it is certainly a most appropriate time to pray in tongues when you are carrying a heavy burden. For praying in the Spirit is to pray in the will of God. You don't know what you are saying. You don't know how to pray. So praying in tongues fills the gap wonderfully.

This means there are at least four times you can know you are praying in the will of God: (1) when the Spirit reveals what the will of God is as you pray (1 John 5:15); (2) when you pray the Lord's Prayer; Jesus said when you pray, say, "Our Father..." (3) when you ask for wisdom (James 1:5); and (4) when you pray in the Spirit (Rom. 8:26–27; Jude 20).

What a fantastic fringe benefit of being a Spirit-filled Christian!

For further study: Romans 8:22–34; 1 Corinthians 14:1–25; Philippians 1:9–11; Jude 20.

Glorious Holy Spirit, what comfort it is to know that You intercede for us and Your prayer is perfect, just as Jesus's prayer is at God's right hand. Increase my faith that I might rest in You when I pray with sighing and groaning and live by the faith of Jesus. In His name, amen.

_____

_____

_____

_____

_____

_____

_____

_____

_____

_____

_____

Day 40

THE HOLY SPIRIT WILL AWAKEN THE CHURCH

I N THE PARABLE of the ten virgins (Matt. 25:1–13) Jesus describes what the state of the church will be like in the very last days: *asleep*. This parable is based upon an ancient Middle Eastern wedding— very unlike our weddings today. The wedding took place not in a church or synagogue but in the bridegroom's home. It could last over a period of several days. The procedure was this: the groom would go to the bride's home and bring her back to his home where the wedding took place, but the bride never knew when he would arrive. Strange as it may seem to us, sometimes he would come in the middle of the night! The bride had young maidens around her who carried lamps. They would need flasks of oil in order to keep the lamps lit in case the groom came at night.

In the parable there were five "wise" virgins; they took oil with them so their lamps would never go out. The wise represent those who were pursuing their inheritance. You will recall from an earlier chapter that every Christian is called to enter into his or her inheritance. Some do; some don't. The five "foolish" virgins took no oil; they represent those who did not pursue their inheritance. In the parable there was a cry at midnight—not 12:00 p.m.; the Greek word means "middle of the night." The cry went out, "Here's the bridegroom! Come out to meet him!" (v. 6). All ten virgins were awakened; even the wise had been asleep. But the foolish virgins' lamps had gone out, having run out of oil. They pleaded with the wise, "Give us some of your oil" (v. 8), but the wise were unable to help. Those who had the oil in their lamps went in to enjoy the wedding banquet.

An important thing to note is this: a great awakening *precedes* the Second Coming. It will be the greatest move of the Holy Spirit since Pentecost—when the Word and Spirit come together as was experienced in the earliest church. The entire church will be awakened, both those pursuing their inheritance and those not doing so. It will be an awakening that will go right around the world in a very short period of time. Three observations:

First, you don't know you were asleep until you wake up! You also do things in your sleep you would never do if you were awake. It is my view that the church today—in this period of "silent divorce" between the Word and the Spirit—is in a *deep sleep*. We do things we would not dream of doing were we wide-awake. The world does not respect the church, but it does not seem to bother us. There is little or no outrage over conditions around us.

Second, when the great awakening comes—the cry in the middle of the night—we will all wake up! But those who were not pursuing their inheritance will be dismayed and beg for help, but it will be too late. The foolish will not become wise but will remain as they were when the cry in the middle of the night takes place. They will be utterly unable to enjoy this great move of the Spirit; they will only observe it from a distance, from the sidelines. Those who were pursuing their inheritance, however, will be right in the middle of it, enjoying it to the hilt.

Third, this awakening will witness the remarriage between the Word and the Spirit. The gospel will be restored to its ancient power. At last the world will fear the people of God. Miracles such as in the Book of Acts will take place, including people being raised from the dead. The blindness on Israel will be lifted; many Jews will be saved. Many Muslims will be saved as well. But at the same time great persecution will take place. I'm sorry, but it won't be all fun.

I asked a charismatic leader in England, "Which do you think the charismatic movement is, Ishmael or Isaac?" He replied, "Isaac." I then asked him, "What would you think if I told you that the char-ismatic movement is Ishmael?" He said, "I hope not."

In my final chapter in *Holy Fire*, "Isaac," I suggest that all we have seen up to now is best described as Ishmael—for whom God had a great purpose. But Isaac is coming! And as the promise to Isaac was a hundred times greater than the promise to Ishmael, so what is coming will be a hundred times greater than anything we have seen! When I first made this declaration at Wembley Conference Center in London in 1992, it was not well received. "You call us Ishmael," charismatic leaders said to me. But some of these same people have come around and have since endorsed what I said. And yet I had no idea that Smith Wigglesworth prophesied the same thing three months before he died in 1947. You can google him and read it for yourself. In a word, he predicted that the greatest move of the Holy Spirit ever seen— eclipsing the Welsh and Wesleyan revivals—will take place; the Word and Spirit will come together!

I close this book with a comforting yet sobering word: the great awakening is at hand, even at the doors. But not all will enjoy it—only those who have faithfully pursued their inheritance. The Holy Spirit will awaken the church. You can count on that. The call will come when we are in a deep sleep—not expecting it. When that moment comes, it will be too late for those who were not pursuing an intimacy with the Holy Spirit to enjoy the next great move of God. I would like this book to be a mini wake-up call to the reader before the great wake-up call comes. It will be too late for the foolish to become wise then. But it is not too late now.

May the blessing of God the Father, Son, and Holy Spirit be with you all. Amen.

For further study: Matthew 25:1–13; Luke 12:35–40; Ephesians 5:8–21; Revelation 3:14–22

> *Most gracious Holy Spirit, I welcome any wake-up call that will bring me to my senses. Grant me not to miss the joy and glory of what is coming. Wake me up now that I may know I am truly pursuing my inheritance. And glorify Jesus to the greatest degree. In His name, amen.*

_____

_____

_____

_____

_____

_____

NOTES

Day 1
The Holy Spirit Is God

1. "Holy Spirit, Truth Divine" by Samuel Longfellow. Public domain.

2. "Holy Ghost, Dispel Our Sadness" by Paul Gerhardt. Public domain.

3. "Lord God, the Holy Ghost" by James Montgomery. Public domain.

4. "Spirit of God, Descend Upon My Heart" by George Croly. Public domain.

5. "I Worship Thee, O Holy Ghost" by William F. Warren. Public domain.

Day 5
The Holy Spirit Gives Warnings

1. To read the text of Jonathan Edwards's sermon "Sinners in the Hands of an Angry God," visit Christian Classics Ethereal Library, http://www.ccel.org/ccel/edwards/sermons.sinners.html (accessed January 15, 2014).

Day 7
The Holy Spirit Gives Talent

1. Deborah Kotz, "Get Happy, and You'll Live Longer," *U.S. News and World Report*, December 17, 2006, http://health.usnews.com/usnews/health/articles/061217/25happy.health.htm (accessed January 15, 2014).

2.　See Charles Spurgeon, "The Sword and the Trowel," sermon preached December 1, 1870, http://www.godrules.net/library/spurgeon/NEW9spurgeon _b29.htm (accessed January 15, 2014).

Day 14
The Holy Spirit Does Not Forsake Us

1.　The late Dr. Peter Eldersveld, radio preacher of the Back to God Hour, was known to make this statement.

Day 30
The Holy Spirit Will Predict the Future

1.　R. T. Kendall, *Why Jesus Died* (Oxford, England: Monarch Books, 2011).

Day 31
The Holy Spirit Will Glorify Christ

1.　"O for a Thousand Tongues to Sing" by Charles Wesley. Public domain.

The Holy Spirit...

Greater than your theology, bigger than denominations,
beyond all we can imagine, God's gift to the church and to you.

Discover more about the most misunderstood member of the Trinity,
and experience His presence in a deeper way than ever before.

"A LANDMARK BOOK"
–FROM THE FOREWORD BY JACK HAYFORD

HOLYFIRE

A BALANCED, BIBLICAL LOOK
AT THE HOLY SPIRIT'S
WORK IN OUR LIVES

R. T. KENDALL
BEST-SELLING AUTHOR OF TOTAL FORGIVENESS

ISBN: 978-1-62136-604-1

CHARISMA
HOUSE